BORN IN

WHAT ELSE HAPPENED?

RON WILLIAMS

AUSTRALIAN SOCIAL HISTORY

BOOK 10 IN A SERIES OF 30
FROM 1939 to 1968

War Babies Years (1939 to 1945):   7 Titles
Baby Boom Years (1946 to 1960):   15 Titles
Post Boom Years (1961 to 1968):   8 Titles

BOOM, BOOM BABY, BOOM

Published by Boom Books. Wickham, NSW, Australia
Web: www.boombooks.biz
Email: email@boombooks.biz

Distributed by Woodslane Pty Ltd. Warriewood, NSW.
Phone: (02) 8445 2300. E: info@woodslane.com.au
© Ron Williams 2018

Creator: Williams, Ron, 1934- author.
Title: Born in 1948? : what else happened? / Ron Williams.
Edition: Premier edition
ISBN: 9780995354906 (paperback)
Subjects: Nineteen forty-six, A.D.
 Almanacs, Australian.
 Australia--History--Miscellanea--20th century.
 Australia--Social conditions--20th century.

Cover image: National Archives of Australia A1200, L11216, PM Ben
Chifley; A1200, L11258, Tea break; A1200, L7788, Rail transport;
A1200, L10855, Boy milking; A1200, L11015, Egg checking line.

TABLE OF CONTENTS

IMPORTANT PEOPLE AND EVENTS

King of England	George VI
Prime Minister of Oz	Ben Chifley
Leader of Opposition	Bob Menzies
Governor General	William McKell
The Pope	Pius XII
US President	Harry Truman
PM of Britain	Clement Atlee

Winner of the Ashes:

1938	Australia 1 - 1
1946 - 47	Australia 3 - 0
1948	Australia 4 - 0

Melbourne Cup Winners:

1947	Hiraji
1948	Rimfire
1949	Foxzami

Academy Awards, 1948:

Best Actor	Ronald Coleman
Best Actress	Loretta Young

PREFACE TO THIS SERIES

This book is the 10th in a series of books that I have researched and written. It tells a story about a number of important or newsworthy Australia-centric events that happened in 1948. The series covers each of the years from 1939 to 1968, for a total of 30 books.

I developed my interest in writing these books a few years ago at a time when my children entered their teens. My own teens started in 1947, and I tried to remember what had happened to me then. I thought of the big events first, like Saturday afternoon at the pictures, and cricket in the back yard, and the wonderful fun of going to Maitland on the train for school each day. Then I recalled some of the not-so-good things. I was an altar boy, and that meant three or four Masses a week. I might have thought I loved God at that stage, but I really hated his Masses. And the schoolboy bullies, like Greg Favel and the hapless Freddie Bevin. Yet, to compensate for these, there was always the beautiful, black headed, blue-sailor-suited June Brown, who I was allowed to worship from a distance.

I also thought about my parents. Most of the major events that I lived through came to mind readily. But after that, I realised that I really knew very little about these parents of mine. They had been born about the start of the Twentieth Century, and they died in 1970 and 1980. For their last 20 years, I was old enough to speak with a bit of sense. I could have talked to them a lot about their lives. I could have found out about the times they lived in. But I did not. I know almost nothing about them really. Their courtship? Working in the pits? The Lock-out in the Depression?

Losing their second child? Being dusted as a miner? The shootings at Rothbury? My uncles killed in the War? There were hundreds, thousands of questions that I would now like to ask them. But, alas, I can't. It's too late.

Thus, prompted by my guilt, I resolved to write these books. They describe happenings that affected people, real people. In 1948, there is some coverage of international affairs, but a lot more on social events within Australia. This book, and the whole series is, to coin a modern phrase, designed to push the reader's buttons, to make you remember and wonder at things forgotten. The books might just let nostalgia see the light of day, so that oldies and youngies will talk about the past and re-discover a heritage otherwise forgotten. Hopefully, they will spark discussions between generations, and foster the asking and the answering of questions that should not remain unanswered.

The sources of my material. I was born in 1934, so that I can remember well a great deal of what went on around me from 1939 onwards. But of course, the bulk of this book's material came from research. That meant that I spent many hours in front of a computer reading electronic versions of newspapers, magazines, Hansard, Ministers' Press releases and the like. My task was to sift out, day-by-day, those stories and events that would be of interest to the most readers. Then I supplemented these with materials from books, broadcasts, memoirs, biographies, government reports and statistics. And I talked to old-timers, one-on-one, and in organised groups, and to Baby Boomers about their recollections. People with stories to tell came out of the woodwork, and talked no end about the tragic, and funny, and commonplace events that have shaped their lives.

The presentation of each book. For each year covered, the end result is a collection of short Chapters on many of the topics that concerned ordinary people in that year.

I think I have covered most of the major issues that people then were interested in. On the other hand, in some cases I have dwelt a little on minor frivolous matters, perhaps to the detriment of more sober considerations. Still, in the long run, this makes the book more readable, and hopefully it will convey adequately the spirit of the times.

Each of the books is mainly Sydney based, but I have been deliberately national in outlook, so that readers elsewhere will feel comfortable that I am talking about matters that affected them personally. After all, housing shortages and strikes and juvenile delinquency involved **all** Australians, and other issues, such as problems overseas, had no State component in them. Overall, I expect I can make you wonder, remember, rage and giggle equally, no matter whence you hail.

INTRODUCTION TO 1948

WWII ended in 1945, and the mood of the population had changed since then. For the first year or so, there were strong feelings of relief and of sorrow. There was sorrow because almost everyone had lost a son or brother or dad or uncle or friend. Many people had lost many such loved ones. Many more still had been crippled or wounded, or had loved ones severely damaged. All of us had spent years separated from the people we loved, and wanted to be with, and none of us knew who would ever come back. The legacy of those years would make people sorrowful for years; indeed, even now they make many an oldie sit down and ponder.

There was clearly relief. All the dangers of war were gone, and things and people could get back to normal. Soldiers were coming home, mums and dads were back together, lovers were re-united. Children, the lucky ones, had their family together again. It was so wonderful, to be home, or to have them home. As Vera Lynn sang "Willie will go to sleep, in his own little room once more." The world was full of joy and hope, and despite all the austerity and rationing that still pervaded, it seemed that this world was indeed a great place to live.

By the end of 1947, Australia had become a good place. Granted, it was also an irritating place, because all those ration coupons were still needed to buy most things. And there were still lots of things that could not be bought, although if you had a bit more money, **the black market**, by some miracle, could get most things. But these were just irritations. Everyone knew that some day, in the time of the never-never, they would go away, and then they would have to find something else to grizzle about.

But the focus now was different. There was still no way of forgetting the past, but life had to go on, and it was the future that people were thinking about. They were settling into long-term jobs, finding long-term partners, crawling to bankers to get long-term mortgages. And saving to get the cars, and Hills Hoists that every new home-owner wanted. Of course, it was not all plain sailing, because, for example, the bankers were hard-hearted, and new or old cars could scarcely be bought. Buying a block of land needed lots on money, and lots more of eating red-tape. We all know that life was not meant to be easy, of course. Well, in early 1948, it was **not real easy**, but there was the realistic prospect that it would get better.

All of this nest-building came with the inevitable. Namely, the Baby Boom. In 1940, the number of births in Australia was 70,000. By the end of 1947, it was 120,000. And it kept rising. For example, in 1951, it was 240,000. **What an increase**. It moved this nation quickly out of the slow lane, and helped to change the dynamics of our entire society. Not everyone agrees that all of the changes were for the better. How many people have I heard say that they long for the days when you could leave your doors unlocked? What about scooping the cream off the top of the milk that turned up every day on the front verandah? There were good things about the past, and yet the Boom years brought a whole raft of good things too.

So, in the early part of this book, I will talk about the goods and bads that were still looming at the start of 1948. **Firstly**, I will talk about a few of the carry-over issues from last year. Then I will add just a few examples of the intrusions and controls that officialdom still placed on the populace.

After that, I will go on to the main part of the book and write about the major events in 1948, and mix them in with much trivia and many ideas that also tell you a lot about the period.

ISSUES FROM 1947

The Communists in Australia. The Reds here fell into **two categories. The first** wanted **a full-scale revolution along the lines of the Russian Revolution in 1917**. There, the Tzar and aristocracy all lost their heads in a bloody revolution, their castles and property were seized, and the goodies were shared among the proletariat. Profits were appropriated by the State, and personal conduct was subject to much official scrutiny and control.

The second faction of Reds wanted a similar State but **without the revolution**. They thought that their end could be achieved by working within the laws of this land and that the changes could be more gradual.

The **revolutionary faction** never gained much of a following among Australians, and their influence in **elections** was almost nil. But, they did get control of most of **the tough Trade Unions**, and they then worked to cripple the State by leading the workers into thousands and thousands of pointless **strikes** over many years.

1947 was the year when these Unions felt their muscles growing. During the war, it was regarded almost as treason for workers to go out on strike. After all, could anyone justify striking if it meant that some of whatever you produced would be denied the men fighting overseas?

Could anyone justify **not** producing coal, **not** working the wharves, or **not** shearing sheep if it meant that our lads overseas might die as a consequence? Of course not, and not only our Federal Government but the man in the street agreed.

This created a capitalists' paradise. Capitalists and bosses were able to impose working conditions on the workforce that would never have been accepted before the war. For example, in 1942, the normal Christmas break of two or three weeks for all the toiling classes was, in that year, forbidden, and the break was cut down to two days. There were thousands of other instances where the workers were dudded by the bosses in those years.

But those years had now gone, and our proletariat wanted better conditions and many also wanted revenge. Here the Reds in the Unions came in. **They had this wonderful old weapon called the strike.** They were prepared to use it at **the drop of a hat**, and the masses were happy to go along with them.

So, by the end of 1947, strikes were being called everywhere right across the nation. No warning, no time frame, and for no real reason, other than to cripple the nation and, for a few avid Reds, to cut the heads off our politicians.

STRIKES AND POLITICS

Bob Menzies was the Liberal Leader of the Federal Opposition. He was a cultured, deliberate, thoughtful man with wonderful powers of oratory. By 1947, the Labor Party had held the reins of government for about seven years. So Menzies was faced with the worrying task of finding a way to get rid of an incumbent Labor government headed by the popular, though very conservative, Leader Ben Chifley.

Menzies quickly realised that the Communist Party's activities could be exploited. Both the Communists and Labor espoused the socialist state, though the Reds were more extreme in their expectations and were certainly

much more extreme in how they would create their new revolutionary State.

Despite their differences, both of these Parties were unified in the support they gave to the process of striking. This was a wonderful folly that **Menzies was happy to exploit**. And exploit it he did. **He flogged Labor** with the taunt that it was in bed with the Reds. He crowed that Labor and the Reds were just different factions of the same Party that wanted to socialise and nationalise everything in life. He associated Labor with International Communism, and Russia, and Reds in China that were just then successfully ending their revolution. In all, he warned us that **the Reds were really bad, and their fellow-travellers were the Labor Party**.

It was great politics, though it was all scarcely true. Yet in 1947 he boosted his anti-Red message, and tarred Labor with the same brush, into a constant tirade, and he kept it up until he retired almost 20 years later. Any time he wanted a boost at the polls, be talked about "**Reds under our bed**s" and his ratings immediately went up.

The end result for our purposes was that strikes were already an integral part of life by the start of 1948. In this book, I will not keep talking about them, but I ask you to keep in mind that they were there in the background each and every day, and there were only a few Reds and Pinks who got any pleasure out of them.

A NOTE ON RATIONING

Behind war-time rationing was the idea that, with so many of our men overseas, this nation could not produce all the goods that it needed. One way round this was to reduce the amount of stuff that we consumed. So, every man, woman and child in the nation was issued with a number of coupons that they could use when they purchased goods. **When the coupons ran out, nothing more could be bought.** For example, six ounces per week of butter was the most that anyone could buy. And so on for every major type of goods you could think of.

The only exception to this rule was where **a black market** developed. There you could buy almost anything if you had a bit more money than the normal price. As time went on, the operations of these markets became more and more sophisticated, and the volume of money that went through them grew greatly. Of course, they were quite illegal, and the authorities tried to stamp them out. But, they were out of their class, and the black markets thrived.

MY RULES IN WRITING

Now we are just about ready to go. First, though, I give you a few Rules I follow as I write. They will help you understand where I am coming from.

Note. Throughout this book, I rely a lot on reproducing **Letters from the newspapers**. Whenever I do this, I put the text in a different font, and indent it a little, and make the font somewhat smaller. **I do not edit the text at all.** The same is true for the *News Items* at the start of each Chapter. That is, I do not correct spelling or grammar, and if the text gets at all garbled, I do not correct it. It's just as it was seen in the Papers.

Second Note. The material for this book, when it comes from newspapers, is reported as it was seen at the time. If the benefit of hindsight over the years changes things, then

I might record that in my Comments. **The info reported thus reflects matters as they were seen in 1948.**

Third Note. Let me also apologise in advance to anyone I might offend. In a work such as this, it is certain some people will think **I got some things wrong. I am sure that I did**, but please remember, all of this is only my opinion. And really, **my opinion does not matter one little bit in the scheme of things. I hope you will say "silly old bugger", and shrug your shoulders, and read on.**

OFF WE GO

So now we are ready to plunge into 1948. Let's go, and I trust you will have a pleasant trip.

JANUARY NEWS ITEMS

The Liquid Control Board **managed the supply of petrol from the distilleries to Service Stations**. Every Station **could receive new supplies only when they handed in an equivalent number of petrol coupons collected from motorists....**

Yesterday the Board singled out a Service Station in Melbourne's St Kilda, and suspended its license to sell. It said that the Station had handed in **a high proportion of counterfeit coupons,** and pointed to regulations requiring them to check coupons for validity....

It is well known to everyone other than the Board that counterfeiting has been going on for years. In any case, **it can be expected that the Board will now make it a burning issue**.

Jews from Europe were still flooding into Jerusalem. Mainly they were people who had survived the German persecution of the wartime years, and who found that there was no chance of rehabilitation in their own devastated nation. So they were keen to settle **in the new nation of Israel that right was now in its infancy**....

The citizens of Palestine did not want these new settlers, and were in active military-style resistance to them. **At the moment**, 20,000 Arabs had surrounded 1,400 Jews trapped in the old part of Jerusalem, and had spent four days intent on starving out the Jews.....

At the same time, British armoured cars attempted to capture Arab snipers who were appearing at random and shooting Jews. As soon as they killed one sniper, another opened up. 45 Arabs were killed in a small village by a Jewish raiding party. The above is a small sample. **The violence would go on and on....**

We shall hear more about this as we proceed.

A young girl in London lost her eyesight three years ago through meningitis. This week, the **cornea of one of her eyes was grafted** onto the eye of a DFC war-hero in an operation. It will be **three weeks before the world knows if such an operation can successfully be done.**

Our laws stipulated that t**he prices of second-hand cars should be pegged** at the levels set by a Government Department. These pegged prices were well below what the average would-be motorist was likely to pay....

So, it was not a surprise to hear from the Automotive Association of NSW **that last year not one in a hundred second-hand cars sold at the pegged price....**

The Secretary of the Association said that "**only a fool or an honest man would sell at the pegged price**". The whole idea of a pegged price was a war-time effort to keep prices down. Clearly, **it was time to drop the pegging**. But also clearly, there would be bureaucratic resistance to doing so.

In New Delhi, **Mahatma Gandhi was shot and killed.** He had just finished one of his hunger strikes when he was assassinated in the street. Death was immediate. The nation entered into deep mourning, and even his bitter political rivals mourned his passing. **India was on the verge of gaining independence from Britain.**

REGS, RULES AND LITTLE HITLERS

In this Chapter, I will talk about rationing and restrictions and the consequences that flowed from these. In my earlier books, I have spent some time telling how crippling they were, and I sometimes think that I have exhausted the subject and should stop writing about them.

But, I can't do that. **They are still here.** It you want to buy meat, or butter, or clothes, you can only buy them if you have enough coupons. If you want to buy almost anything, you have to wait for weeks or months until you come to the top of the queue. If you want to sell your house, or buy a car, you need permission from Canberra, and you will realise how long **that** took.

So, I can't ignore it. Instead, here, rather than repeat the weighty treatises of my earlier books, I will just ramble through a few current quirky instances of the broad issue of rationing and restraints and shortages, and leave you to shake your head at the world we lived in, and thank your lucky stars that we all survived.

First, though, I want to explain to you that there was a good reason why so much interference was foisted on a population that had already had enough. It all goes back to the war years when this nation was in real peril of Japanese invasion. The Labor Government correctly saw that we **could survive only if we adopted tough austerity measures**, and we accepted all sorts of rules and regulations that allowed government to direct our every action.

There is no doubt that this policy worked. Now, with the war fading into memory, the ordinary citizen wanted the government to do some fading of its own, and give back the freedoms that had been temporarily suspended. Not everyone agreed to this.

In particular, **the Labor Party** had seen how effective State control had been during the war, and it wanted to continue those controls. **What it said was that it wanted a socialist State, and that measures such as nationalisation of industries were the way to go.**

As a part of this, **the system of regulations**, that it had built up, should stay. Despite increasing pressure from the slowly-awakening population, it dragged its feet in reverting to the pre-war freedoms, and sought at the same time to keep tens of thousands of bureaucrats in comfortable public service for as long as possible.

The examples below give you **a January view** of some of the irritations that arose as a consequence.

ALLOCATION OF NEWSPRINT

The *Sydney Morning Herald* (*SMH*) said that, from today, it would reduce its circulation by 70,000 copies. In response to **the shortage of US dollars**, only essential goods could be brought from the US, so newspapers round Australia are being forced to reduce consumption of newsprint by 58 per cent. Newsprint is the paper that is used for printing.

Persons who have ordered home delivery would still get them, but **papers would not be available for casual sale through newsagents and paperboys**. The size of the *Herald* would be reduced by 59 pages per week, but "although some cuts in content in the news coverage is inevitable, the *Herald*, in accordance with the policy it has consistently followed since restrictions were first introduced, has preferred to restrict its advertising, and sacrifice its sales."

Also, in accordance with reductions in font size, the standard page would have nine columns instead of eight. The final column of Page One, full of trivia, would, however, still be called *"Column Eight"*, even though the page would have nine columns.

RABBIT CONTROL

Rylands Brothers stated last night that Australian production of fencing wire and wire-netting (including nails and barbed wire) was now at the rate of 18,240 tons a year. Prior to the War, production had been six times as great, at 112,000 tons. "There is a large lag in production that is getting larger. Right now, it would take eight years of production to wipe out the deficit in orders."

Mr Neil Barrett, of the Wheatgrower's Union, said that primary production could come to a standstill, if we cannot have fences. We must have an immediate increase in production if we are to survive. "Are we to become the nation of the great unfenced? Should we surrender the bulk of the nation to the rabbits, and simply fence ourselves into the cities?"

CLEAN OUT OF SOAP

The *SMH* scratched its head about why, given that the country produces so much tallow, there should be such a shortage of washing soap, and the toilet variety is getting scarcer and scarcer. It points out that a short while ago, waterside workers took the bull by the horns, and imposed their own ban on the loading of tallow bound for overseas.

The situation did not improve. A bit later, the price here was increased to encourage traders in soap to deal in **this** country. Again to no avail. Perhaps it could be that tallow dealers are **hoarding** the material in the hope of a further price rise. Whatever the reason, the present situation is "fantastic". The black market strikes again.

Comment. In 1950 I can remember still washing myself using bars of Sunlight soap. The soft and delicate, scented, coloured, soaps that Colgate sometimes provided were available only on the black market five years after 1945.

NIGGLES FOR THE HOUSEWIFE

Letters, P Thomason. I suppose I am only one of the many housewives who would be glad to see rice once more in the shops.

But what puzzles me is this: How is it that we can buy all the ground rice we do not want, but not a grain of whole rice? If rice is so scarce, why go to the expense of grinding it and selling it cheaply at about one third of the price of sago and tapioca. We want the whole rice, the ground rice does not lend itself to many dishes.

Comment. The shortage of rice often stirred housewives into writing to the papers. We had not yet learned to use rice like our Asian neighbours, but it was still nice to have the occasional rice pudding at the end of the Sunday meal.

The trouble was that we grew very little rice ourselves, and all that we **did** produce was committed to go to Britain and other countries of the Empire.

Special Court, Punchbowl. A woman butcher was fined 275 Pounds in the Rationing Court today, because she had failed to account for **two and a half million meat coupons** in the last eight months.

Investigation showed that 2,221,485 pounds of meat had been killed and sold. The lady had done the paperwork for none of this, nor had she supplied any coupons. Subsequently, 1,439,739 coupons had been tracked down, but over a million are still outstanding.

Mr Collins, SM said that this was one of the most serious cases to come before him. It showed complete disregard or defiance for the law.

Comment. It was not much fun buying meat. You could guarantee that you would have to wait 15 minutes or more in a queue, then that the meats and the cuts you wanted were rarely there. Then if you found something that you would eat, there was a delay while customers waited to have their coupons collected.

The good lady butcher above would have served half a dozen customers with their meat, and then have gone through the tortuous business of collecting their coupons. This involved counting down a dozen coupons in each coupon book, then cutting them out with scissors, arguing with some customers that about the numbers taken, and finally collecting the money. Meanwhile, queues developed.

But she found a way out of this admin stuff. She did not collect coupons.

DRIPPING WOES

Letter, E Pickard. The ban on **the export of dripping** in any food parcel is iniquitous and unnecessary. For years, I have been sending eggs packed in dripping to seven different families in England. I save this dripping, and collect it from friends, as otherwise it would be thrown out as it now will have to be.

A personal aside. In those days, meat such as sausages, steak, and chops, used to come with a healthy quantity of fat attached. And they were cooked in dripping. Now, I am afraid, it is impossible to get decent meat, and **I can only get fat-free stuff that has no taste at all**. How I long for a meal of greasy bacon and eggs with a nice fatty cutlet, and a sausage with fat oozing out of the fork marks. All cooked in last month's retained dripping, with all those flavours of past meals. And, of course, covered in salt.

TOBACCO AND FAGS

This nation had no indigenous tobacco industry, so all of our products were imported. When the war came, there was no official rationing system for these products, so the wholesalers from overseas simply sent out supplies to the industry and let **it** dole out the product under any system it devised.

But, of course, prices were fixed, so that a huge black market trade developed. If you had the money, you could always get your roll-your-own or your cigarettes. If the tobacco-shop owner wanted to preserve some semblance of normal or fair trade, he doled out a little bit to his loyal customers.

After the war, this system still persisted into 1948, even though the rest of the world then had oodles of tobacco. The Government was still not importing tobacco from overseas because it did not want to spend our precious US dollars on frivolities. But, it started to allow the importation of English tobacco, because of our special relationship with Britain.

Not everyone was satisfied.

Letters, J McNamara. To conserve our US dollars for the purpose of keeping the economy sound, restrictions on the import of many things are necessary, but it is wrong to penalise **smokers** without their consent. The scarcity of tobacco is causing an undercurrent of **discontent amongst industrial workers, and production suffers**. The whole thing is proving to be penny wise and pound foolish.

English tobacco and cigarettes are now plentiful, but they are a poor substitute for the familiar brands we know, and are too dear. Normally, I would spend about six shillings a week on familiar brands, but today I can spend fifteen shillings a week, and still feel as though I haven't had a smoke.

Letters, Harry Cohn. What a silly world we live in. Tobacco from England it brought in to this country. And we gratefully smoke it. Let me ask you, though, just where in England is their tobacco industry situated?

Let me answer for you. There is no tobacco grown in England. They get most of the supplies that they send to us from South America. So it goes from there to England, then to us in Australia.

Why do this? It is so that we do not use up our scarce US dollars. But if we bought directly from South America, we would not use any US dollars at all. Let me ask you another question.

Why do we do this? The answer is that we have bureaucrats who want to keep their jobs doing worthless work. And it is because we have a socialist government that wants to buck the forces of history and keep us permanently on a war-footing. Shame on them.

SOME OZ-BRITAIN RATIONING PROBLEMS

News Report, *SMH*. The Australian cricket team will be sailing next month on the *Strathaird*. **The team will eat**

English rations while in Britain, because it does not wish to have an unfair advantage over the British while on tour.

The Board of Control also does not wish to deplete the stocks of meat available to the citizens of Britain, so it is sending a supply of Australian meat with the team. A food bundle of 12,300 tins of meat is being sent to the British Food Ministry. They estimate that this will be equal to the amount of meat that the team gets through in England. The food was purchased by an appeal through the Food for Britain appeal. Don Bradman will formally hand the food over to the Ministry.

Comment. The arithmetic or the reporting is a bit astray. This works out at about 800 tins per player, over about three months. That is, about 9 tins per day. That is a bit too much, even for the barbarians from the Antipodes.

Bundles for Britain. In the 1946 book in this series, I wrote about the massive amount of free food and materials the ordinary Australian citizen voluntarily sent off to a starving Britain. This aid went on, and on, into 1948. At times, there were lots of problems. Sometimes, the British Post Office confiscated parcels because senders had not stuck precisely to their pedantic labelling. Sometimes, there were complaints about the high cost of postage. Then complaints about non-delivery. But through all this, the Australian public simply shrugged off the difficulties, and in a truly magnificent manner, maintained the aid.

Now in 1948, was it any different? Were they tired of giving, was their attachment to Britain waning? The answer is a categorical "No". Bundles for Britain were still sent at a great rate. **The easiest way** nowadays was to visit **some specialist shops**, and order and pay for one of many hampers that you could choose from. Then leave it to the pros. But no matter how it was done, there were tens of thousands of people still sending bundles three years after the War had finished. The clipping below illustrate a few aspects of this.

> **H Simpson, Food for Britain.** The Fund is sending 20,000 food parcels to Britain a week, Mr Simpson said last night. Since the express delivery system was started five months ago, 300,000 parcels have been sent. Each pack now contained at least **a tin of condensed milk, fruit in syrup, steak pudding, camp-pie, dripping and honey, and a packet of butter-scotch**.

INSPECTORS IN THE MEAT INDUSTRY

Every government department wanted to see to it that its regulations were working well. They could do this in many and varied ways, such as good forms-design, and making their rules known by advertising. But in the long run, they relied on a generous number of inspectors to police the citizens and prosecute them if necessary. Of course, there were the ordinary inspectors like those on the railways who charged you if you did not have a platform ticket, and truant inspectors who nabbed kids wagging school. But there was a vast horde of others, who swooped on more serious lawbreakers, and these unfortunates found their names in black print in the newspapers.

As we have seen above, the meat industry had its rules, and it was also lucky enough to have a battalion of inspectors to enforce them.

A Weir, Special Prices Commissioner. Yesterday, thirty inspectors, disguised as buyers and carters raided the meat markets in Sydney, and arrested three men.

The first of the men sold 12 lambs, 12 brains and five frys for 23 Pounds, instead of the regulated price of twenty Pounds and seven shillings. The second had similarly sold meat, properly priced at nine Pounds, for the massive mark-up of ten Pounds. These two were each granted bail of 100 Pounds.

> **Prices Branch.** The Prices Branch have recently conducted enquiries into the pricing of meat in butchers shops. As a result, 31 prosecutions will be launched today. Another 17 warnings will be issued.
>
> During the enquiries, inspectors visited hundreds of shops in 44 suburbs in city areas. All sorts of meat and rabbits were found to be overpriced. For example, one piece of bacon, that should have cost seven shillings and nine-pence, was sold for ten shillings. A special squad of twelve inspectors will continue to check Sydney's meat prices.

Notice that the price was fixed for every type of meat, every cut of meat, and every bit of offal. Notice too the zeal of the inspectors. "Of 13,972 cases of overcharging reported, all have been fully investigated." The advert does not say that "a sample" was investigated. It says "all", and that they were "fully investigated." Imagine the manpower involved in doing that.

So, here is another factor to consider when looking at the removal of controls. There was a vast horde of inspectors earning a good living who were likely to lose their jobs. Not just in the meat industry, but in most others as well.

FEBRUARY NEWS ITEMS

A Hollywood movie called *The Outlaw*, starring **bosomy Jane Russell**, was released in Australia a few weeks ago. A Catholic priest in Brisbane is trying to have it **banned in his suburbs because it exposed too much of her breasts**. It was banned by the Catholic Legion of Decency in the US....

The theatre proprietor said that he would **continue to show it because it was not banned by Federal authorities**, and so it must be decent. He thanked the priest for the extra publicity he had generated for the film.

During the war it became obvious that **we were short of population**. The size of our armies was vastly limited by our shortage of men. After the war, it was agreed by all that we needed "**to populate or perish**" in a world where invasion was seen to be a distinct possibility. Our **young people bonded together and sacrificed themselves** to create a wonderful baby boom. But we needed migrants as well....

So **assisted passages were offered to thousands of Brits.** They were really just getting under way in 1948. It was announced that 6,000 assisted migrants were expected to come to New South Wales this year. **500 of them would be nurses**, who were classified as our most urgent requirement.

In Minnesota, USA, a storekeeper was refused a beer license by the local Council. The man left the meeting, and returned with a deer gun, and **shot and killed three Councillors.** He then shot himself.

Comment. Gun violence in America is not new.

A crocodile escaped from the Zoology Department of Sydney University and is free in Sydney's crowded Chippendale area. It is an experimental animal, and **must be kept in a hungry state**. The following police description was issued. **"Length: three feet. Age: indeterminate. Colour: grey. Eyes: amber. Expression: fierce"**....

Any person who encounters the beast should not feed it, but rather notify the police immediately.

Don Bradman, aged 40, announced that he **will retire from all cricket** after the upcoming tour of England. He will play his last Test in Australia, against India, later this month.

TB was a disease of the lungs that was reaching **epidemic proportions** here, even though we had a relatively high standard of living. Various medical bodies were investigating whether the vaccine known as **BCG** could be used effectively to combat TB in Australia....

Research in Britain had produced positive results, and it was now hoped that a laboratory in South Australia would be able to produce **enough supplies to make large scale trials in Australia possible**.

Comment. It took five years, but **TB was virtually eliminated here by vaccination with the BCG.** In many regions, the vaccinations were made mandatory.

BIG BROTHER

In 1948, George Orwell wrote his famous book, *1984*. Part of the drama of the story came from the theme, later to become a slogan in the early Fifties, that *Big Brother is watching you*. In fact, in Australia, Big Brother, namely the Federal Government, had been watching for almost a decade, since the beginning of the War.

In this Chapter, I want to look at a few industries where the vigilance was pervasive, and at the same time, caused maximum concern to average Australians. Of course, there were some regulations that the average person could shrug off with a grunt and a shake of the head. For example, the ban on **pink** colouring in the icing put on cakes.

But others affected everyone and nagged at them all the time. So, I want to examine these, and at the same time look for signs that *the times they are a'changing*, and that maybe the authorities might have to adjust quite soon.

THE CAR INDUSTRY

Cars were still very difficult to buy in early 1948. For new cars, potential buyers were required to make application to the Federal Government, stating their reasons for wanting the car. These were sent to State Offices and Canberra, and there they were sorted out by public servants. This means that "special consideration" was given to certain classes of persons. At the top of the list were disabled returned servicemen and ex-servicemen **setting up businesses**. No one will be surprised to know that there were many such persons suddenly wanting to branch out on their own.

Then there were primary producers, particularly those living a long way from a railway station. Finally, the medical profession, including ambulances, and those engaged in essential work, such as housing projects. Apart from these, the normal citizen simply had to wait till he crept up the queue.

This, however, was no small wait. At March 1948, Eddie Ward, the Minister for Transport, announced that there was a waiting list of **45,000 outstanding applications**, and that this figure was growing at 4,000 per month. He added that 18,000 permits to buy would be issued this year. So, by my arithmetic, at that rate, **the person at the bottom of the list could expect to buy a car in about three years**, if there were no other persons getting "special consideration."

The Acting Director of Car Transport said today that he was tightening the system used in issuing permits for people to buy new cars. Many prosecutions will be launched **against dummies who got a permit and sold it to other persons.** He indicated that he simply could not understand that it seemed that some people were prepared to make money out of the car shortage. He said the extent of the **use of dummies had just been realised by his Department**, and that some dummies may have applied for quite a few cars, using fictitious names, and different addresses.

He went on to say that in future, successful applicants for permits **would be notified by telegram**, to speed up the process. Some journalists noted that this would cut the average wait time from three years right down to three years less one day.

In March, Ward said that **in future**, the applications from NSW would be processed by **Federal** Public Servants, instead of NSW Servants as was now the custom. This was because NSW was short of the senior resources to do the job. Ward went on to say, in his typical helpful fashion, **that people who have already lodged applications, will have to submit new ones on a new form, and sign a statutory declaration.** No arrangements were to be made for personal interviews, and all business would have to be conducted by correspondence.

Comment. The first of these clippings **makes you wonder just who the dummies really were**. The Letters pages had been constantly reminded of the use of dummies and other devices for jumping the queue, and now the Government Officers say that they had **at last** realised that it was going on. In the second clipping, the arrogance of the Minister and his officers was typical of the attitude that these inspectors displayed towards the public.

Rackets in old cars. Older cars could be sold locally, but **only at the official price published by government. Selling above that price was illegal, and punishable.** This process was wide open to abuse, and criticism of it was widespread.

Letters, I Cahill, Chamber of Automotive Industries of NSW. I have utmost respect for the law, and the greatest admiration of for the law-keeper. But it is my opinion that, with new vehicles in such short supply and no prospect of any appreciable improvement in the position, it is foolish to sell a used car in good condition at the price pegged by regulation. This is not to suggest for one moment that, if the vehicle must be sold, the law should be broken in effecting its disposal. Rather do I suggest that the Prices Branch should revise the scheduled prices, or abandon the regulations which in their present form have proved to be not enforceable.

Some vehicles I know are being sold by honest people at pegged prices, but these instances are rare. The fact is that a regulation lacking realism and feasibility has caused otherwise honest and honourable people to become cynically dishonest.

Letters, DISTRESSED. An advertisement in the *SMH* last week read "Fiat 1928 Tourer, Pegged Price: 320 Pounds. Will accept 320 Pounds". Yet another, better car, a 1940 Chevrolet, 12 years younger, was pegged lower by four dollars. The paper was full of these anomalies.

Is it possible that the people who govern can be so stupid as to be oblivious to the fact that price control on used cars has been a complete failure, and is treated as a joke by all. Price control on all new commodities may be essential, but when applied to second-hand articles such as used cars, it is impossible to arrive at a fixed figure.

It is estimated that 99 per cent of the public break the law when buying or selling any used car later than a 1932 model. As a dealer who has specialised in the sale of used cars for the past 20 years, and who is now **not** in business solely due to this very unfair regulation, I state definitively that the sooner price control is placed in the hands of someone who knows the true position, the better it will be for the public in general.

By February 1948, the pressure on the bureaucrats reached a peak. They sprang into action, and issued a statement, that promised "drastic regulations" in a battle of wits between officials and black marketeers. The *Sydney Morning Herald* editorial greeted this promise with scorn. What, it asked, is the purpose of keeping the prices of old cars down at an absurdly low level? Why should two cars of the same make sell at the same price if one of them has been battered, and the other one is in perfect condition? It looked like control for control's sake. **And just plain jobs for the boys and girls.**

A few weeks later "drastic new regulations" were released by the Prices Commissioner, Mr McCarthy. **It turned out that they were not all that drastic.** A number of vehicles made between 1927 and 1933 were re-classified, so that there were now only 3,000 classes instead of **the 4,000 classes previously**. And there was a provision that if a vehicle was in "an exceptionally good condition", the seller **could apply to Canberra** to charge a higher price. Mr McCarthy assured everyone that the schedules of second-hand prices were in fact a bit higher than the trade opinion of the value. It just happened that the laws of supply and demand came up with a different value from the theoretical value that McCarthy calculated.

By the time February came around, there was a new element entering the Letters. It turned out that about then, a reasonable number of new cars from Britain were entering Australia, and so hopes of getting a car came out of never-never land. Suddenly, people were talking about why we need regulation at all, and about how much it costs, and asking what purpose does price fixing achieve?

Letters, Frank Murray. In a few months, if things keep going the way they are, we will have plenty of new cars, and that means there will be a follow on to plenty of old cars. Prices will come down, and people will be able to get what they want.

Also, it will release lots of heavy-handed bureaucrats and inspectors from their jobs, and we can then hire them to wash our new cars. Of course, they would have to get a licence first to do the job.

Letters, Frank Posetti. It seems that we are getting a lot of new cars from Britain. This can only be regarded as a benefit to the nation. For too long we have sat here and read about the large number of cars freely available in England, and at the same time we keep sending them parcels of food for free. I have long argued that they should, in return, go in to bat for us, and force the powers that be to send us cars in return.

Now, they are coming anyway. I believe there is also some talk that we will make new cars here in Australia later this year. So, it looks like things are picking up. So now we should start getting rid of all the blood-suckers who are making a fortune out of car buyers, and that includes the black marketers and the Canberra lot.

But you do not get rid of the Canberra lot so easily. They announced in May that they were about to **go back over all outstanding applications for permits** to make sure that **all those who claimed to be business persons in fact really were.** They stated that they had found that when confronted with statutory declarations, and the likelihood of heavy fines for deception, **many people recanted**, and accepted being put back to the bottom of the list, without any "special consideration."

So, at this point, it seemed that **the heavy hands of the bureaucrats were still firmly in place**.

But, **to the surprise of everyone**, events over the next few months moved quickly, and major changes and improvements were made to most systems, starting in June. **I will keep you waiting in suspense till then.**

THE LIQUOR INDUSTRY

The whole industry was heavily regulated. Prices in pubs and clubs were fixed for all products, and opening hours were mandated. In night clubs, the number of seats, and where they were placed, and what types they could be, were all controlled. Every part of the industry was under control, with a fierce system of inspection. I will try to give you a scant glimpse of all this with a single court record.

Special Court, Margaret Street, Sydney. Norman Davis was fined forty Pounds by Mr Addison, SM yesterday. He had been found guilty as owner of a restaurant, of selling a bottle of beer for the price of four shillings, instead of the list price of one shilling and seven pence. He later sold a second bottle, also for four shillings. The owner argued that the bottles had been ordered beforehand, and so he had added a service charge. The SM was not impressed, and pointed out that, even as a service charge, the price was excessive. The restaurant was fined 10 Pounds.

INSPECTORS IN THE BACKYARD

The system of inspectors was **not restricted only to the big end of town**. It got right into the backyard of every household. I mention two that riled me at the time, even though I was just in my teens.

The first was the inspectors **who came round to check wireless licences.** Every **wireless** had to be licensed, and pay about one Pound per year. Later, it was softened a little, so that every **household** had to have just one licence. In any case, these busy bees walked the streets now and then, at least once a year, and looked for aerials. When they saw one, they would pounce and demand to see the bit of paper that was needed in order to use such a luxury. Failure to produce the licence resulted in a fine. I was young enough at the time to think that this was a Nazi-style invasion of households. Actually, I still think that.

The second one was chook inspectors. Every household was allowed to have chooks in the backyard. But 18 was the upper limit. Again, persons would walk the streets and look for chook sheds. Then they would go in and check the number in each. If you had more, then a fine would result. My thoughts at that time were that the nation was crying out for more eggs, and so we should be encouraged to have more hens. I suppose I overlooked the need for proper sanitation in yards. But it did feel good to have another set of inspectors to rail against.

Comment. I was not the only one, who by 1948, was fed up with this system of being all the time responsible to petty regulations and being fined for breaches. Everyone was sick of it.

Why was it, three years after the War was over, that price-fixing and other restraints were still in place? You could argue that it was necessary to preserve our national fortune, and too much spending would reduce that fortune. Or that if we spent too much, we would run out of dollars, and go broke. Or that the more we consumed, the less we would have to send to England.

All of these might have had some element of truth, but by now, people were tired of them. They just wanted to get on with their lives, and stop looking over their shoulders.

NEWS AND VIEWS

David Jones advertised the advent of pressure cookers. They promise a chook **done in thirty minutes,** and later ones cut the time even further. Hold one handle still, and rotate the other. Do not lose the little jiggler that goes on top of the steam outlet, because without it, the whole apparatus is just another saucepan. This was a true revolution in the kitchen.

British Moving Chain Restaurants. A great innovation for the restaurant industry has been developed and patented in **Britain**. The new product is the conveyor belt cafeteria, where customers sit on a conveyor belt, moving at 5 feet per minute. While moving, they are served a three course meal. They begin with soup or another entrée, and after five minutes move into the main meal section. Ten minutes later they will be moved into the sweet and coffee section. The time periods are based on studies which have determined that 20 minutes is the average time for a three course meal. Designers say this new form of cafeteria will eliminate queuing delays and save time and space.

This, of course, was a different world. **Britain** was desperately short of food, and even those people who could afford to eat out were constrained by the shortages of supplies and by food rationing. These in turn limited what could go on the menu.

Right now, in Australia, how would restaurants survive if the meal was over in twenty minutes? It takes longer than that to get a waiter. And in any case, much of the profit comes from alcohol sales, so there are good incentives to keep customers waiting for quite a while.

News report, *ABC*. A revolutionary new device has been introduced for the first time to Kingsford Smith Airport, at Mascot. It is a piece of technology, developed during wartime to spy out the locations of enemy aircraft and naval vessels, and is now being introduced for peaceful purposes. An operator traces the track of an approaching aircraft on a radar-receiving screen. The track is reproduced on a special screen in the control tower, enabling the control officer to guide and advise incoming pilots. It is estimated that the **use of radar in Australia will become widespread if this innovation is successful**.

Photo Finishes. The first Australian horse race, in which the winner was decided by a photo, was run today. Up till this happy time, decisions were made about who won simply on the say-so of three judges. And there were many who doubted the full integrity of every judge at race tracks round Australia. Hence the need for cameras.

Bad news for campers. When Christmas comes to Australia, half the population pick up sticks and head for the water on beaches and lakes. Half of them end up in a 12 by 12 tent canvas tent, **in makeshift camping grounds** within a few feet of the fish and water....

The **authorities are now intent on stopping this** because of "poor sanitation, fire danger and inadequate accommodation". Cabins will need to replace tents, and for dedicated campers, accommodation will be provided at serviced sites in National Parks....

But in any case, holiday tent villages are doomed.

MARCH NEWS ITEMS

The **Queensland Labor Premier** got a bit carried away. The Railways and others were on strike, crippling the State's commerce and, he said, some parts of the State were running short of food. In dramatic moves, he said that **strikers would be sacked**, he imposed **censorship** on news and radio, and he spoke of the need to "**avoid all elements of civil war**...."

His stance was ridiculed on all sides. Even the **Labor** Trades and Labour Council described his measures as Fascist-like, and called on him to resign. He responded with an attack on **the Communist Party**, which he blamed for the strikes, and described them as mimicking Molotov....

For the record, let me note that **there was no civil war** in Queensland in that period.

The war was over, and women were keen to get some colour and style back into their lives. Thus, when the **"New Look" arrived, from Paris, women flocked to the city stores** for a glimpse or a purchase. The frocks had plenty of flair, yards of material in the skirt, and a longer skirt in the day, but shorter for the night.

Comment. It looked better than the grunge and slacks of the war years....

But, wait a minute. Good times are really here for women. The Government has announced that for the next two months, women will only **have to cough up five clothing coupons for a frock.** The normal number demanded is eight. This short-term reprieve is because cool weather has left retailers with large stocks.

Some men are having a sartorial holiday too. Royal Ascot racecourse in England, where the Royal family gathers occasionally, has decided that in these austere times, men will be admitted to the Royal Enclosure **dressed in lounge suits**....

Of course, **morning suits are preferred, but** if shortages of cloth and coupons makes this impossible, then lounge suits will be accepted.

Can you believe it? The Feds announced **new regulations to control the car trade**. They placed price limits on a huge classification of **spare parts**, and on **the tools** needed to make repairs. These moves will help to control the black market in the car trade, **they say**.

Arthur Calwell, Minister for Immigration, **struck again**. Australian soldiers were in Japan acting as a peace-keeping force. Calwell decreed that **no soldier who married a Japanese girl could bring her to Australia....**

Nor would any child from the marriage be allowed in. "It would be the grossest act of public indecency to allow a Japanese person of either sex to **pollute our shores...."**

It was accepted that the **Japanese were still hated from the war**, but this punishment of Australian soldiers serving overseas was seen by many as **being heavy-handed**, to say the least.

SOCIAL ISSUES

A number of social issues always disturbed our society. Sometimes they were pushed into the background. But often they flared up to become vexatious matters that the full population was discussing.

FALLING BIRTH RATES

In January, 1948, the *Sydney Morning Herald* carried an interesting Editorial. It was responding to some comments made by Dame Enid Lyons, the wife of Joe Lyons, who, before his death in 1939, had been Prime Minister for much of the 1930's. Dame Enid had been elected to Parliament in 1943, and became Australia's first woman Senator. So, when she spoke, some part of the population listened to her.

The Editorial talked about the problems that households faced in that year. It says, by way of introduction, that most people agree with the contention that the strain on most mothers in housekeeping is the main cause of falling birth-rates. It points to the housing shortage as an irritant, and to the shortage of domestic help. Also, it cites "shopping is harder, prices are higher, and services are scarcer; and she gets no 40-hour week."

Then it gets down to more tangible causes. Falling birth-rates can partly be attributed to "broad social and spiritual changes." Among these is the tendency to live in small houses and flats, and no longer in the large multi-generation household. It also lists the decline in the practice of religion, and "the erosion of family life by outside entertainment." Finally, the **"anxiety of modern women to remain youthful"** is lumped in the same sentence with the unrest caused by international problems.

It turned to Dame Enid's theme. She argued that birth-rates were falling, and proposed that the solution was the imposition of **strict restraints on the sale of contraceptives**. Apart from the fact that she was absolutely wrong in her population statistics and forecasts, her comments point to an issue that bedevilled the nation for years to come. Dame Enid was a Catholic, and that institution took the lead in the fight against contraceptives.

But there were many other individuals and organisations that also opposed their use. Any young man at the time will tell you how embarrassing it was to approach a chemist for these devices. The ABC, two years earlier, had issued **a decree against discussion of sex matters, including contraceptives, on air.** Sweeping this issue under the carpet did not help anyone. Dame Enid's comments did not open up public discussions much at all, and **the taboo against talking about anything to do with sex, religion and politics stayed in place for at least another decade.**

TUBERCULOSIS

TB was still on the march. In my 1946 book, I pointed out that the incidence of TB was growing in the population, and that the authorities were generally slow in moving to counter it. I have re-visited TB now because, first of all, TB had increased further in Australia and was an even greater problem than before. And secondly, to draw attention to the very different treatment regimes that had developed across the States.

I need to correct myself immediately here with respect to NSW. There was, in fact, **very little development in that State in those two years.** The Sydney Morning Herald ran a series of articles that pointed out the deficiencies in the TB system in that State.

It said that the shortages of beds and nurses were as bad as previously. It claimed that nurses were hard to get because of the fear that they had of contracting the disease, and because the treatment of patients in sanitaria was a humdrum matter, with wards full of suffering patients slowly deteriorating till death. Wards were vast and airy and cold, and nurses' quarters were poky and run-down, and the food was boring.

Beds were in short supply, waiting lists for surgery were up to two years and patients often died before getting to the operating table, no preventive medicine was administered, and diagnosis was haphazard, and late, and often useless. Patients received a trivial sum of money to support their families. And patients were often complaining that **they** got butter with their meals in the sanitaria, while **their families at home** could not afford it.

This list of inadequacies could readily be doubled. It shows no change, in effect, from 1946. In **NSW**, that is. The reason for presenting it here is to **contrast the situation with that in Victoria**. There, the system had developed so that in all respects it had improved vastly on NSW. I will not go through all the improved features one by one, but will instead just highlight a few.

Victoria had begun voluntary x-rays in 1943, and had backed them up with a substantial awareness campaign. Over 1,000,000 persons had now been x-rayed. Examinations were free, the machines could handle up to 1,000 persons per day, and two mobile vans were available to service country areas.

All school children were being tested using the new Mantoux Test, and where a positive was obtained, the family and even the school bus-driver was also examined. All school teachers were x-rayed at appropriate intervals, and hospital staff were using the BCG vaccine, which later was to become almost universally effective.

Importantly, financial arrangements were improved, and a successful scheme to keep patients in their own home was operating, with adequate finance. The shortage of sanitarium beds was nowhere near as acute as in NSW, and in several country areas, day-clinics took the place of beds in institutions.

The system in Victoria was experimenting, trying to find a solution to the whole problem. NSW had broken the problem down to its little parts, and was doing something, not much, to fix all of these problems as if they were not related.

These problems with TB went on for over another decade. But later incidence figures over that period show that Victoria hit on solutions much quicker than NSW. Remember, this meant the saving of thousands of lives.

MENTAL HEALTH

In 1948, the term mental health had a much narrower definition than it does today. This was in the days before depression became a "disease", and before drugs were widely used to sedate and restrain patients. It was in the days when people were put into asylums, and were **declared**, sometimes officially, "mad", and were often forgotten even by their relatives. But caring civilians and professionals periodically got their views heard about the faults in the treatment handed out, even though it must be said that their entreaties generally fell on deaf ears.

In early 1948, the NSW Minister for Health, Jack Kelly, started a small controversy with his remarks about restraining mental patients.

Letters, J Patchett In his statement denying that there is cruelty in asylums, Mr Kelly is reported to have said that "some patients had to be restrained because they were a danger to themselves, other patients and nurses." He went on to say that these patients were fastened by canvas, and that this is a practice employed by asylums all over the world.

This statement is incorrect. I was employed as a male nurse in England from 1932 to 1946, in three different asylums, and I have never seen that method of restraint employed on any type of patient, no matter how violent he became. Furthermore, any type of mechanical restraint was abolished from asylums in England more than 25 years ago.

Any of the nursing staff of an asylum in England using any kind of mechanical restraint would be instantly dismissed. Mr Kelly would obtain further proof of this from the "English Lunacy Laws."

Letters, Nurse. I was gratified to read your article calling for interest in those who are mentally ill. Angels from heaven could achieve little under present conditions of overcrowding and shortage of staff.

If we had more psychiatry blocks in public hospitals and more rehab hospitals in the country (well staffed), it would relieve the congestion in the large mental hospitals, and minimise the restraint that is often needed with staff shortages and overcrowding.

In these days, when nurses take general, obstetric and mothercraft trainings, not a great many have time and inclination to add a mental course. But we need our nurses to get some knowledge of mental training during their general training, and this is now lacking.

I know too much to criticise those who are struggling with the problems inside our institutions. They know that they need more space and more staff. We want institutions that will cure, and not just be dumps.

Letters, RETIRED. After 40 years as a mental attendant in NSW hospitals, I know of no better method of controlling a violent patient than using a camisole of gloves, not only for his own protection, but for the safety of other patients and staff. Take away restraints, and a rough and tumble ensues every time the patient requires attention. It would be interesting to know the method your correspondent, Mr Patchett, would introduce to handle a really acute mania.

Nurses and attendants in NSW are forbidden to place a patient under restraint without orders from a medical officer.

Letters, ex Female Nurse. I would be interested to learn from Mr Patchett what means were used in England to restrain difficult mental patients.

I was employed in one of Sydney's largest hospitals which did not use straps. I had a deep love for my patients, and I see no cruelty in the use of such restraint, provided that the patient is treated with the gentleness and affection that a good nurse deems it her pride to give.

Comment. Mental health nowadays covers depression, youth suicide, all sorts of manias and phobias. Back in

1948, the definition was not so encompassing. But then, as now, it was an area that was not afforded much attention. Everyone, from governments right down to the man in the street, put it into the "too hard" basket. All of these problems mentioned in these letters, and many more, plagued mental health for decades, and still do. At times it has flared up to become a major issue. For example, there have been, over the years, violent arguments over sterilisation of patients, over electro therapy, over de-institutionalisation, over use of drugs, and always over shortages of funds and carers. But the problem keeps popping up, and I suspect we are now not much closer to a solution than we were in 1948. For example, suicides among young males and old males and doctors could well receive more attention.

EDUCATION

Now a look at some education statistics is interesting. Firstly, back in 1948, the number of youngsters who sat for the end-of-school exam was 6,000. Seventy years later, the number was 60,000. This is a tenfold increase, while our population has increased three-fold.

Second, in 1948, the percentage who went on from the IC to the LC was twenty percent. Nowadays, it is closer to eighty.

We all know that **the nation is better educated than it was**, but these figures show the extent of this improvement.

INFANTILE PARALYSIS

Infantile Paralysis was just now becoming an epidemic.

Nine cases of polio were experienced in Sydney within 12 days. Fearing an epidemic, Metropolitan Medical Officer of Health, Dr Grahame Drew issued a number of warnings. Dr Drew said last night any person who had been in contact with a child suffering paralysis should remain isolated for about three weeks. Further, that any children who were sick should not be allowed to become fatigued, their temperature should be taken daily, and a doctor should be called if there is even a slight rise in temperature.

This polio scourge gripped the nation until the late sixties, when the use of the Salk and Sabin vaccines became widespread. Up until that time, every parent worried, and scurried to the doctor, whenever a first symptom appeared. Even now, in 2018, there are still a few people alive round the world who have spent all these years in an iron lung.

HAZARDS OF CAR TRAVEL

In 1948, many cars were open sided, with just leather-type material flapping round to protect from the weather. Also, of course, there was no air conditioning. So, a lot of vehicles were, rather gloriously, open to nature.

News item, Maitland Mercury. A bee today caused a car crash. The bee flew into the moving vehicle, causing the driver to lose control as he attempted to dodge the bee. The car swerved off the road, and plunged down a 30ft gully, one passenger being flung free in the process. Nobody was seriously injured. The bee appeared to escape, also without apparent injury.

NEWS AND VIEWS

Whale Steaks for Oxford Rowers. The Oxford rowing eight have been given whale steaks to supplement their meat ration. It was reported that their rowing-practices alone consumed more calories than they got ration coupons for. Thus, the whale steaks were necessary in order to avoid injury to the rowers. In response to this, rival Cambridge bought a cow at a local farm, which would be milked by members of their club.

Remember boys diving for coins? At most wharfs round the nation, at holiday times, boys of all ages would stand about on the edge of the wharf, and dive down to collect coins that tourists would throw in. It was good fun for all, but not without its dangers.

Manly local paper. Max Prior, aged 15, swallowed two pennies and a halfpenny, put in his mouth for safety, while diving for money at the Manly wharf yesterday. He was taken to Manly hospital for X-ray treatment, and later to the Royal North Shore Hospital for an operation.

Trowel Shortage: Mass production of bricklayers' trowels began in Australia, at Gyrex Products. Previously, trowels had only been obtainable from overseas, and had been in serious shortage since the beginning of the war. The shortage was estimated to be between 30 and 40 thousand trowels.

Problems with beer. Wollongong Hotel Ban: In 1947, a referendum had been held in NSW to ask if the hotels could stay open till 10 o'clock at night. The answer was that they could not, and so the State was stuck with the six o'clock swill and stand-up pubs for years.

Agitation for decent drinking conditions did not stop, and the news was full, all the time, with accounts of anti-publican and anti-breweries activities. This article below is a single sample.

Wollongong workers unite. Last night, a meeting of unionists placed a black ban on all Hotels in the greater Wollongong area. The ban will not be lifted until the local publicans meet a number of demands. They are required to keep open during all legal trading hours, sell full quotas **over bars** at legal prices, allow a committee to inspect cellars and hotel records to ensure all quotas are sold, and ensure there will be no victimisation of employees.

OFF TO LONDON

Before the growth in air travel that was about to occur, the most common way to go was via ship. The send-off was generally a grand affair, with families at the wharf, lots of tears, and champagne if you could get it, promises and more promises that letters would flow back and forth every few days, vows of fidelity, and miles and miles of streamers. Wonderful days.

It was also possible to catch a sea-plane. These normally carried only about 30 people at the most, and had a smaller range. That meant that **there were more frequent stops and stop-overs**, and they virtually had to island hop.

They often took **two weeks to get to London**, though faster flights were available for business travellers. Several old-timers who flew this trip have suggested that **the revival of such services today would be very popular with leisurely tourists.**

APRIL NEWS ITEMS

When the war in Europe ended in 1945, thousands of German officers and Nazi officials were **spontaneously hanged** right across Europe by local lynch mobs. Later in 1946, the Nuremberg Trials were officially held, and many of the top German leaders met a similar fate. But **trials went on**, and many nations tried hundreds of perceived villains **over the next few years**....

For example, in early April in a US War Crimes Court, 12 former officials of German arms manufacturer Krupps **were acquitted** of "having conspired with Hitler to fight an aggressive war." **But they were not free.** They have yet to answer charges of having "abused slave labour and exploiting occupied countries"....

It was generally true that **those who were charged were found guilty of some crime or other**.

Norman Yardley is captain of the England Cricket team. His local county team is Yorkshire and he is proud of that. His wife is pregnant, and **they have decided to move back to live in the Yorkshire local area.** That is because, if the child is a boy, **he can play for Yorkshire only if he was born in that region**.

The Post-Master General said that he was **not interested in the development of television** in Australia until the **back-log in telephones** had been fixed. At the moment, this nation had **outstanding applications for 120,000 phones**. And, in fact, we did not get TV for another eight years, just in time for the 1956 Melbourne Olympic Games.

Only a few nations of the world yet had atomic bombs. The US, Britain and Canada, and the French and Russians were in the so-called "Atom Club." Many of our leaders were anxious to join the Club, and **a few years later Bob Menzies would bend over backwards to gain entry**. Many of these leaders thought that if we could provide the scarce uranium ore to the Club, then our chances of joining would be greatly improved....

So **our explorers were now offered handsome rewards** if they discovered and reported finds of the ore from any location in Australia. Over the years, many such finds were recorded, but despite this, **we were never admitted to the Club.**

The Western Australian Government **has received a cheque for 18 Pounds from an American tourist** who was here with a touring party "some years ago." In their trip to the outback, a **"goose or a swan" was shot**....

Now the tourist from New Hampshire "wants to be clear of **all moral obligation in the matter**. Our party wants to be absolutely square on this matter with your Agriculture Department and the Commonwealth." Hence the cheque.

I have to hand an invitation to attend **a community sing-along** in the Scout Hall at Dungog on April 15th, 1948, at 8pm. I am asked to bring a plate, and also my own voice. Songs will be old-time and modern....

In days when **entertainment in the bush was hard to find** at night, weekly **Community Singing and local concerts were always popular**.

REDS AGAIN

In my 1947 book, I wrote a few pages on how the Communist Party in Australia was becoming prominent in the trade union field. The bad publicity it had been getting carried over into 1948, and the Liberal Party and all employers and newspapers were blaming it for everything.

The Party had got itself into prominent positions in all the major unions, and was using the strike weapon time and time again. And politically, many of them were keen on socialising everything, and making Australia into a replica of Russia. So, they had a lot in common with some sections of the Labor Party, who were also keen on socialism, and hence the Labor Party was not nearly so critical of the Reds.

In 1948, the Reds really became conspicuous, both at home and abroad. **Our local Reds were completely innocent of the events occurring overseas** and, while many applauded them, many others looked askance at them. Also, at home, there was a split between some conservative Reds, who wanted to introduce moderate socialism by peaceful parliamentary means, and the firebrands who actually wanted a revolution and the enforcement of full-scale Communism. **I will start with the overseas events**, and then come back to Australia.

The overseas developments occurred against a background of rapidly increasing hostility between the Western world, led by America, and the Soviet Union, soon to be enlarged into a formal Communist bloc. All of the small States, like Czechoslovakia, and Poland, were soon to become Russian satellites, through various forms of Russian intervention. The Soviet idea was to create a ring of subservient nations around its own borders so that they would provide a buffer against any aggressor. America wanted to frustrate Russia in this, because it thought that, one day, it might be that aggressor.

THE RED COUP IN CZECHOSLOVAKIA

The Government there was a coalition of half a dozen Parties, of which the Communists were about one third of the total. They were in an uneasy truce with other Parties, all of which had banded together to eradicate the Germans towards the end of the War. In late February, 1948, elections were due to be held, and it seemed that a mighty shift in power would occur.

The problem for the non-Communists was that **the Communists were much better organised than they were**, and were undoubtedly very good at rigging elections. So, the leader of the Government, a non-Communist, tried to engineer an early election before the Reds could get into election mode. He organised for twelve of his ministers to resign, expecting that this would precipitate the early election. But now **the President simply appointed Communists to replace the gentlemen who had resigned**, and ended up with a new government with his own Red choices occupying the key positions. As simple as that, democracy was finished in Czechoslovakia for fifty years.

This pattern established the norm for Russia and its satellites. If a rogue group or nation felt that it wanted to leave the Communist sphere of influence, and fermented a rebellion, the Russians put their foot down. This always involved sending in troops and tanks, and then the execution of some of the rogues and the imprisonment of many others.

The Western world complained about it, and passed resolutions against it all in the UN, but to no avail. After all, Russia could always veto anything that was bad for her, and she had plenty of satellites that would always vote for her.

So, the pattern was established, and the use of it, and the threat of it, kept Russia safe from attack, and at the same time, **left her free to meddle in the affairs of all other nations in the world. Just as America was doing.** But **we** were in the American camp, so when the propaganda machine had its say here, it was the Russians who were the baddies, and our reaction was **always to look on Russia as a monster who was hoping to consume the world**.

BERLIN BLOCKADE

After the Germans were defeated in WWII, post-war Germany was divided into four zones that were to be respectively under the control of the British, French, Americans, and Russians. **Berlin, in the centre part of Germany, thus had to be in someone's zone, and in fact it was in Russia's. Then Berlin itself was also divided** into four similar zones. Access to the so-called Western Zone was via two railway lines, a traffic highway and several roads, and canals and three air corridors.

Big trouble **started** brewing in January, 1948, when the Russians insisted on boarding trains to inspect the passports of German passengers. Then, a major signal was sent in April, when two rails links were cut, and some canals. But in June, the Russians took drastic action, and cut off all remaining land communication with the West, by rail, road, and barge. This left West Berlin with **only one way to get**

materials in or out, and that was by air. The famous
Berlin Blockade had arrived. Two and a quarter million
West Berliners had to be supplied by air. Or, if not that, the
Western powers could move out of Berlin. This was high
drama indeed.

Within a few days, the West had decided that **an airlift
of food and materials was possible**, and had started to
implement this. The air corridors into the beleaguered
city were crowded with British and American planes that
landed every few minutes. In all, while the blockade lasted,
2.3 million tons of materials were flown in. **Over 200,000
flights flew in. The blockade lasted almost a year, and
was lifted in May 1949.**

Again, here we see the international Reds posing a threat
to the wishes of the Western World. Mind you, despite its
seriousness, it was all well stage-managed. The Russians did
not close the air corridors, and in fact maintained radar and
air traffic controls that the aircraft needed for the twenty-
mile trip into Berlin. A number of other services, such as
water supplies, that were in the Russian sector, were kept
running to provide for the Westerners. No one wanted to
escalate into a war, and everyone was careful to make this
plain. But the Russians learned that the West, when push
came to shove, was determined not to be bullied. And the
West had a sample of the lengths that Russia would go to
promote her interests.

Still, there were anxious moments. At times, a few American
die-hard generals threatened to storm the barricades, and
lead armed forces through the blockade. **There were
periodic artificial scares about the Third World War**

being imminent. But these were just part of the political posturing that was going on, and soon went away in favour of another pose.

More serious were things like unemployment.

News reports, Berlin. Electricity cuts imposed yesterday could cut down 98 per cent of Germany's industrial activity. This would result in 375,000 persons being thrown out of work. The cuts in electricity have occurred because coal stocks have just about run out, and the remainder will have to be used to provide food and essential services like water supply. Radio stations have been forced to close down, and newsprint shortages have severely reduced the sizes of those papers that are still publishing. Authorities have equipped hundreds of trucks with loudspeakers to tour the city to broadcast essential messages.

The Allies plan to counter the unemployment problem to some extent by putting 10,000 people to work immediately to clear up bomb debris in the city. It is hoped soon to increase this number to 40,000. Persons who remained out of work would be paid unemployment relief, of about sixty per cent of normal wages.

REDS IN AUSTRALIA

Back in Australia, these events were watched with misgivings, but with the attitude that every thing was too far away to be really worried about it. Other events with the Communists were happening at the same time. **Yugoslavia** had been taken over by **Marshall Tito**, and while he did not endorse full links to Moscow, he was a dictator closer to Moscow than to the Allies.

The Reds were also active in China, and in South-East Asian countries like Malaya. So all of these were of concern, but **it was the activities of the local Reds that stirred people**. Here, they led hundreds of Trade Unions out, on thousands of strikes. We talked earlier in this book, just how successful they were in staging these disruptive activities. But, I should mention that there was where their success stopped. They made almost no headway in gaining power through the ballot box, and socially they had no influence at all. But the correspondence flowed into the papers about local matters. Every newspaper was deluged by Letters that denounced their activities, and a sample is included below.

Letters, E White. When are we going to get something more effective than cheap talk to dispose of the menace of Communism. Those famous people who believe that its suppression is a suppression of free speech should realise that freedom for them is analogous **to freedom to wreck our economy and eventually our nation. Known Reds should be gaoled** for criminally assaulting the law and order of the community, as many others are for far less heinous crimes. Let every country town and suburb have a public meeting asserting its views on the matter.

Letters, G Milgate. The passive minds of the Chifley Government, drowsing in their pipe dream, are reducing Australia to a Communist's playground of organised scarcity.

Rather than make the Communist Party illegal, it would be safer to prevent them from holding any office in any Union. For violations a penalty of 500 pounds should be imposed, and a fine for the Union of 1,000 pounds. Deny the Commo the right to control any club or association. We want active democracy, with wide-awake ideas that keep the ship of State afloat.

Letters, John Dease. Mr Dease was a well-known and much-respected radio personality.

Your Special Correspondent the Red menace named me as being associated with alleged militant policy of Actors Equity, through my membership as an Executive. He further quoted several opinions charging me with being "actively sympathetic to Reds", and a "subversive cog in the wheel of the Russian Communist Party."

I wish to refute these charges in the strongest possible terms, both as an individual, and as a Senior Vice President of Equity. During my tenure of office, I have always counselled scrupulous moderation in all aspects of our dealings as a Union, and have sought the support of all those of my fellow members who are determined to oppose Equity's functioning as a political body.

While we may regret the passing of the unity and singleness of purpose that marked the war-time years, the return to peace has revived my personal conviction that a man in my job, engaged in public entertainment, must have no association with any political movement which even remotely can be described as partisan. I assure you that my work in Equity is directed towards helping that body to care for the material, cultural, and social welfare of its members, leaving them free to express themselves politically if they so desire – outside.

Letters, L McDougall. It is generally conceded that the world is as close to war today as it was in 1939, and the third march to war in thirty years is most disturbing and distressing. Russia's policy of territorial and influential aggrandisement speaks for itself, whilst the formation and encouragement of an active fifth column stamp Russia as the greatest threat to peace and democracy of all time.

We must deal effectively with the fifth column. The local Communist policy of industrial unrest, created shortages, and the spread of suspicion and frustration, is **part of the Moscow war policy.** The activities of such Communists should be terminated. Such action by the Government would tend to restore public confidence, and check the designs of Stalin and Co.

Letters, John Perry. For many years, certain public men have issued warning after warning against the dangers of Communism, but have been ignored.

By now, it should be obvious that Communism is a very real and potent danger, and if we do not pull together and exert our utmost strength against the insidious enemy, our future existence, so far as our current way of life is concerned, will be in jeopardy. We should all endeavour, by instilling into the minds of those who are still foolish enough to close their eyes to what is happening, the vital necessity to appreciate the danger.

Letters, A Hebblewhite. The People's Union has decided to join with the League of Rights in other States in seeking a Commission of Enquiry into the activities of the Communist Party.

Communism cannot be destroyed by repression as the last ban proved when it emerged more widespread and stronger that ever. It can only be destroyed by exposure, and a Commission of Enquiry would greatly assist the people to understand the viciousness of it.

REDS IN MALAYA

The Reds were active in the region near us.

The two Letters below indicate that Malaya, for example, had its own problems with its own local revolutionaries.

Letters, MALAYAUST. A close-up of Communism in action, such as we see in Malaya today, would sicken and horrify every decent Australian at home, as it does here. Of my many friends who returned to Malaya after three and a half years imprisonment in Singapore during the War, three have been callously shot to death. Day after day, with sickening regularity, we read of still another one or two defenceless Chinese patriots who have been cold-bloodedly murdered. The ruthless extermination of helpless political opponents is a distinguishing characteristic of their revolting ideology.

Letters, H Stokes Hughes, Sungei Estate, Malaya.

I wish that those authorities in Australia who refuse to supply us arms could see how we planters and miners are armed. It is ludicrous to see most of us with a shotgun or revolver try to protect our families against Sten guns in the hands of ruthless Chinese Communist brigands. There are many Australians in Malaya. Most of the mining is done by them, and a fair number are planters. I am one myself, and incidentally, I am ex-AIF of two wars, and I ask my cobbers to help.

REDS IN USA

As a final piece on Reds, let me show you the hysteria generated in America during this period. Mind you, there was worse to come, when Joe McCarthy was let loose in the Fifties.

US Congress. The Chairman of the important Senate Committee investigating Communist spying in the US, said last night that it might be appropriate **to impeach President Truman** because he was actively helping Communists by not revealing names and details of FBI agents that the Committee was asking for. The Committee later suspended its hearings, because it could not get the information it wanted.

Let me add for the record that the President of The United States was **not** impeached for aiding Communism.

OZ RADIO

Australian radio shows were marred by vulgar jokes, horror serials, and Smart Alec announcers, the Parliamentary Standing Committee on Broadcasting was told today.

The NSW Branch of the Committee submitted that evening serials were emphasising murder, violence and crime, as in *Danger Unlimited* and *First Light Fraser*. They also mocked teachers and adult authority, as in *Yes, What?* and *Comic Capers*.

Some services also encouraged young people to emotional excess and morbid hysteria, as in *Romper Room.*

WOMEN JURIES

The Premier of NSW said today that Cabinet had approved the appointment of women to juries.

He added that, because of the shortage of accommodation for these women, the provision would not come into force until a date to be announced.

Leaders of women's groups welcomed the decision. Mrs Jessie Street said "it is a responsibility of all citizens and should be extended to all citizens." Mrs Eleanor Glencross said "Sensible women are definitely needed on juries, especially when cases regarding females are being considered."

MAY NEWS ITEMS

The Shop Assistants Union will be disappointed. It had applied to the Courts to **abolish Saturday morning shopping**. But **the Courts refused their application**. So workers will **still be able to buy food and clothing**.

By mid-May, the British will have withdrawn fully from Palestine. In the meantime, the violence between Jews and Arabs is ongoing, with no sign of a future any different from the past.

The NSW Government, **in response to a power shortage**, has said that inspectors will be authorised to **forcibly enter houses to check** whether restrictions are being observed. Any offence will result in a fine of 500 Pounds. In addition, **any one resisting them will be fined an additional 500 Pounds**. For **pensioners**, that is **two years of pension payments. They think** the penalties are too severe....

There are also bans on the use of electricity in shop windows or for advertising and outdoor lighting, such as tennis courts. For the householder, they include a **prohibition on the use of radiators from 7am to 7pm**.

The Returned Servicemens League decreed that Communists would not be accepted as Members of the League. This was because the Reds were seen as intending to subvert the supposed non-political aims of the League, for the purpose of furthering the political agenda of the Communists. Reds already listed as Members of the League are awaiting the decision on whether they will be expelled....

Since **the Communist Party is a legal entity in Australia**, it is dubious whether the RSL's rejection of Communists will withstand a legal challenge.

Do you know these young women? Joan Baldock, Anne Bardon, Barbara Bertram, Elizabeth Heydon, Mary King, Anne Stark, Wendy Walsh? They were **the Australian debutantes presented to the King and Queen** at a garden party at Buckingham Palace....

Because of **the need for austerity**, there will not be a formal presentation. Rather, the Royal couple will mingle freely among the perambulating girls....

At the time, **most girls in this nation expected to make their debu**t, probably at the local Town Hall. What a fuss and to-do it all was....

My sister made her debut in the NSW country town of Maitland. To get to the Town Hall there, she caught the bus, that ran every two hours, in full party dress, to arrive at eight o'clock. She left at 10 o'clock because that was the last bus home....

She died recently, and among her possessions was the dress and jewellery she wore that night. And, in her diary, the bus tickets.

Fifty-seven valuable prints from the British Council have been loaned to the Queensland National Art Gallery. **They have gone missing....**

It is thought that they have been **put on the wrong train**, probably at Wallangarra, and are now **awaiting collection from some railway Goods Yard.**

STRIKE A LOT

This was a period of constant strikes. The country was fast becoming prosperous, jobs were plentiful, and profits in many industries were good and getting better. On the other hand, wages and salaries had not increased as they should have since the War, and working conditions, which had stagnated during the War, were now under attack as being archaic. Circumstances were just right for strike actions, and the bigger unions obliged on cue with strikes all over the place.

I have divided these into two types. Firstly, there were one-day and two-day stoppages that caused disruption and annoyances, and allowed the workers to let off steam. Sometimes, there were a series of these, as in the coalmines, and over a period of time the effects of these started to impact the economy. Secondly, there were prolonged strikes, lasting weeks or months, that tried to achieve major changes to conditions, and caused major disruptions to many people.

The masters of the **one-day stoppages** were the coal miners and the wharf labourers. The coal miners seemed to be always out, and often this resulted in the newspaper carrying headlines **supposing** that trains would stop, and that there would be no electricity or coal-gas for the cities. The Sydney newspapers were unrelenting in their attacks on the miners. Every day, for years, they carried a front-page estimate of "coal output lost" the previous day. They could equally well have carried totals of mineworkers killed and injured, or miners off through mine-induced illnesses. They could have carried reports of mines closed for the day because a fall of coal had killed workers, and left that portion of the pit unsafe. But they simply reported "output lost."

In fact, in the mines and in most industries, most strikes occurred because of safety issues. For a miner to see a floater twenty feet up in his section, and knowing that once floaters quickly develop they are likely to fall, he has little choice but to walk away. If management says they have to work out the shift and then it will look at it, there is little sensible choice but to strike.

Then there are the demarcation issues. Some of these sound silly. If an electrician is laying wires in a tunnel, and a three-foot pile of coal is in his way, then it makes sense to get a shovel and move it. But, if discovered, this becomes a demarcation dispute, and probably a day's work is lost. Yet if that same electrician feels a bit insecure and puts in a prop himself, then this is dangerous because, believe it or not, a prop must be put in just right. So here the demarcation issue has a valid point. Where do you draw the line, where is the point of demarcation? At the time, it was drawn tightly, with no cross-over of duties, and the big stick was to **stop the pit** when this type of trouble happened.

Then, again in the pits, there were problems with working conditions. Miners by 1948 wanted a hot shower when they came up. In a bathroom with a locker, and not with their clean clothes suspended on hooks from the ceiling, that were lowered down from long ropes over a pulley. They wanted the same bathing conditions that people in 1948's squash clubs had. But it took them years of needling and striking to get these, and other basic amenities.

The wharfies and trammies and others had similar beefs. Those not in government employ could see that capitalists were making good profits, and that they were not getting a share. They could see that their short-term and long-term safety was being ignored and the "fat industry barons" were prospering. So behind all these tangible reasons to strike, there was another one. They wanted a fair share of the money that they were making for others. They wanted a **fair go**.

A good example of **a prolonged strike** occurred in April and May. It all started after Mr Connolly, the President of the beer-makers ULVA, said that **things were looking good for the beer industry**. He quoted higher production figures, with the NSW breweries producing ten per cent more than they did last year, and also that he expected that the backlog would be completely gone by the end of next month. He pointed to some factors that might stand in the way of this happy situation, such as shortages of sugar, problems with the Tasmanian hops crop, and transport problems with strikers in Victoria. But, he said, the public's purse was well filled, **production would be high, and things looked rosy**. He made this statement on the day of the annual breweries' picnic, and I suspect that **the excitement of that grand day loosened his tongue**.

Within a few weeks, workers at the breweries had also realised that the industry was headed for better times, and decided that they wanted to share in them. They issued claims, for better wages and conditions, that were inevitably knocked back, and so all of Sydney's breweries went on strike.

The strike followed the then-familiar pattern. There was a stand-off for a week, then the start of meetings between workers and management. These also always failed. Then some arbitrator ordered a compulsory meeting, and this too failed. By now, the workers were getting short of cash, and the Companies were getting worried, so more conferences yielded a few meaningless concessions and bigger displays of stubbornness. Finally, the Unions involved, realising that the workers were by now out of money, called a mass meeting that approved a return to work. Management promised to give serious consideration to the workers' log of claims, and that was that.

It appears maybe that the strikers lost in this battle. But that is not quite so. They did not get much in the short term, but they sent a strong signal that they could not be pushed around, and they would be back on strike if their demands weren't seriously considered. In short, they missed out in the short term, but did get better conditions in the near future. Of course, it would have been better to have reached this position at a conference table without the strike, but unfortunately, there were lots of tough employers around who would not work that way and, it must be said, many a Union figure as well.

This beer strike had some interesting side effects. The strike lasted 40 days and nights, and thirsty men were without beer for much of that time. Easter came and went without beer, and the Sydney Show was dry.

On the bright side, **milk-bar proprietors** had never had it so good. At lunch time, crowds had been unmanageable. "Most of them did not know what to order, or how many they were supposed to have," said Mr Virgona, of Pitt Street. "My daughter slung shakes at six a minute. Viva the great thirst."

The President of the Temperance Alliance of NSW, the Rev C Tomlinson, said that homes would benefit. Less drinking meant more money at home for other things. "The womenfolk will be pleased."

Doctor H Foley, an alderman with **Burwood Council**, said that in many quarters there had been a switch from beer to wine, and to **drinking** beer like wine, and that was creating a serious health problem. "While the number of charges for drunkenness has fallen, I and many other practitioners have treated many acute and chronic cases of alcoholism in the last few weeks as drinkers switch to the harder stuff."

Professor Harvey-Sutton, Professor of Tropical Medicine at Sydney University, spoke to a Women's Christian Temperance conference. He said that hundreds of mothers whose children had missed injury on the roads, and hundreds of women who had more money to buy food, would heartily endorse a vote of thanks to the strike. He went on to attack alcohol from a number of points of view. "People at cocktail parties are noisy and boisterous: they all talk at the same time, no one listens to anyone else, and their talk is worthless."

Bundles from Britain. Forty eight thousand cans, and 960 bottles, of English beer will arrive today on the P&O motor freighter *Paringa*.

So, here we were with the soul-destroying spectacle of the Great Aussie Drinkers having to get their beer from England. Oh, the shame of it! Still we survived, and happily supplies did get better, work conditions gradually improved until the next beer strike, and workers everywhere girded themselves up and waited until it was their turn to strike. As it turned out in those days, they never had long to wait.

Another aspect of the strikes was that inspectors were sent out round city households to see whether people were using too much electricity or gas. If it was estimated that they were doing so, then penalties were applied, including fines.

Letters, Housewife. Last week, a member of the County Council's "Intelligence Dept" stood on my doorstep and cross-questioned me about my consumption of units, which he alleged was greater than the last quarter. It was ironic, I thought, that I had succumbed to the pleas in advertisements and bought new electrical appliances, and now was being interrogated about the power necessary to use them.

At the same time, I resented the insulting demeanour of the man and the impertinence of his employers. I gathered that my crime was using a radiator, though the man failed to gain admission to my house to confirm this.

Like many mothers, I am willing to compromise for the good of the community, but will not be brow-beaten. With a sick child, and an empty grate, I will use the appliances I have bought. Further, I shall not get a doctor's certificate to permit me to do this. I do not have that type of spare money.

During the last gas rationing period, I queried my account, which was actually larger than usual. The reply was that "the saving is so small that it makes no difference in the accounts." The honour system, as suggested by Mrs Glencross, would surely result in a greater saving than that produced by threats and violence.

Here is a consequence of strikes that no one thought about.

News item, Sydney. Three elderly men, and a woman, all elderly, died separately at the weekend after inhaling gas. All four died in similar circumstances. They had turned on their gas jets, to do some chore. The gas had gone off, due to shortage of supply. But they had forgotten to turn off the jets. So, later that night, when the gas came back on again, it flowed freely, and they all inhaled enough gas to kill them while they slept. One lady, Mrs Johnson, was found with her pet cockatoo, which had also been gassed, and was found hanging upside down from its perch. It had written in its birdseed the message "hell, this house stinks."

HOUSING

By May 1948, servicemen had been home in Australia for about two years. Most of them had started to settle down, and the Baby Boom was under way. One problem with this was that there was not adequate housing for the large number of small families that were covering the landscape. In the ten years prior to this, of course, there was virtually no house building because of the war. And for the last two years, despite some serious attempts by government and private enterprise, there had been more promises made than houses built. But, about now, promises and reality started to get closer together, and a reasonable number of new houses started to appear.

Of course, the houses were nothing like the 25-square 2-level places being built in year 2018. Instead, they were, at the minimum specification, a kitchen, a living room and bathroom, and two bedrooms. The material was generally fibro cement or asbestos cement, and roofs were most commonly galvanised iron. They were paid for by taking out a first mortgage to a bank, and a second, more expensive mortgage, to a hire-purchase company, often owned by the same bank. The terms for the first mortgage spread over something like 30 years.

Humble though they were, it was a proud and relieved family that moved into one of them. Everyone had got sick of living with in-laws, and everyone wanted their own neighbourhood and their own new friends of the same age. Once they got there, the competition with the new Joneses then consumed them for years, and cars and carpets and washing machines and refrigerators, all unheard of by the prior generation, came gradually to the top of the list of desirables. And the little children kept popping up, and added to expense. But no one seemed to mind. To me, looking back and doing my research, the years round 1950 were very busy and very happy, for most people.

However, that is not to say they were idyllic. When they got their acts together, the State and Federal Governments built some dwellings and sold them on to the not so well-to-do. To get these, applicants would put their names and credentials in to an agency, and wait for their name to be drawn out of a big hat. Then, if, they were lucky, they were eligible for a house. Another similar scheme was the Star Bowkett movement, where aspiring owners started making regular financial contributions to a pool, and when they got enough money in, they again ran a lottery to select the lucky ones. Private building contractors built the bulk of the dwellings. Some of these ran small operations, with perhaps two houses per year. Others, in this period of rapidly increasing demand, got big quickly. L J Hooker and Lend Lease got a hefty leg up.

There were, however, a wide range of problems that beset the building fraternity. I include a sample of these below.

Department of Building Materials. Cement production in 1948 will be about 100,000 tons less than the State needs. This means that there will be shortages. The problem is being caused by a shortage of manpower, and indirectly, of coal. There are five plants in NSW that produce cement, and another is due to be opened at Charbon at the end of this year. But the setbacks and irritations to its construction will certainly delay it.

The Department will give priority to direct housing material, though it should be kept in mind that other uses are also important. It is used in tile-making, and is an essential ingredient in the making of asbestos-cement. There is also a large export market that needs to be serviced, lest we lose it. We will not establish a formal set of priorities, but will continue to adjust deliveries depending on the various developments in the ever-changing world around us.

Comment. I should mention that over the next few years there were a number of small scandals, where it was reported that cement was going to some venues that could not rightly have priority.

Squatting was a problem. Any dwelling that remained unoccupied for a length of time could simply be taken over by people who chose to do so. The practice of squatting had grown in war-time England, when bombed-out houses were occupied by other unfortunates whose homes had been completely destroyed. There were various opinions, under various circumstances, about the legalities of this, but the law, when applied, was slow to move, and occupancy sometimes continued for months.

Price fixing of real estate was a source of constant irritation. Since the early 1940s, prices of land and houses had been controlled by the Federal Government, and meant that, basically, the seller had to sell at prices that were decided about 1940, and could not sell for any sum above that. Another part of the price-fixing system was that approval had to be granted from Canberra for buying and selling properties, and this **caused massive delays and ridiculous decisions**.

Letters, Solicitor. How much longer is the public going to put up with the farcical price-fixing of land. Solicitors are wondering **whether there is a single land transfer passing through their offices which does not carry a black-market price.**

Some clients frankly ask how they can best safeguard themselves when they pay the black-market addition to the Valuer-General's valuation. Others say "it would not be honourable" to pay only what the law permits "when the property is worth so much more." Nowadays, clients seldom trouble to hide their black-market intentions, and all a solicitor can do is tell them that if they want to break the law, they cannot expect him to help them to do so.

It might be mentioned that in India, when price controls were lifted, prices fell at once below the previously prevailing black market prices. Surely, it is reasonable to expect that if price control of land was removed, more houses and land would be put on the market, and that there would be more competition, and so lower prices, below the current black market price, would result.

Despite protests such as this, the authorities **now** extended it to new homes. How they would estimate the price of a new house in Condobolin, from an office in Sydney or Canberra, has me puzzled.

Ministry for the Interior. The Minister is investigating a statement, made at the ACT Advisory Council, that a furnished house, advertised for sale in Canberra, had cost 14,000 Pounds to build, although the amount mentioned on the building permit was only 4,000 pounds. He will make all relevant enquiries, and will make a statement later.

Rents were controlled too. The Federal Department of Works and Housing, which administers rent control, said that in the last reported 18 months, across Australia, rent increases had been granted to 5298 persons, 2877 were reduced, and 7336 were left unchanged.

Comment. What a drag. To go to Canberra for a rent increase.

The NSW Premier, Mr McGirr. This gentleman grabbed himself some useful headlines when he burst out forcefully at the Premiers' Conference.

The Post-Master General claimed that there was a desperate shortage of buildings for Post Office needs. Mr McGirr replied, "to hell with the Post Office and everything else, when it's a matter of homes. There is no comparison between needs of people for homes, and the provision of equipment for the Post Office. We have thousands of homes with their skeletons built, but we cannot finish them because of the shortage of materials. **Tents are good enough for Post Office equipment.**

Mr S Bain, of the **Licensed Plumbers Association**, claimed that the NSW Housing Commission was taking an unfair share of building materials. He stated that, by taking 43 per cent of building materials for itself, in an attempt to reach its target of 90,000 houses in three years, the Commission was making it impossible for private builders to reach their targets. "Baths, stoves and sanitary pans are non-existent for us, and galvanised iron baths are just unheard of."

He cited the delays in **securing iron for repairs**. **Number one priority**, new housing: six months. **Number two priority**, government agencies, and heavy industries: 11 months. **Number three priority**, pastoralists, grain silos etc: 17 months. **Number four priorit**y, general repairs without a permit: 28 months.

Comment. It might have been hard for our pioneers a century ago to build their homesteads and sheds. But back in 1948, with all the controls and shortages, it was not all that easy. Just as well the community was feeling relaxed and excited.

THERE ARE GOOD SIGNS AHEAD

During WWII, all big signs on railway stations and along highways were removed, and so too were most street names. This was to prevent Japanese spy planes from knowing where they were.

Now various authorities were saying that **most of the signs were back in place**. If you wanted to get off a train at the right station, this helped.

JUNE NEWS ITEMS

Since the end of the war, our armed services had been deployed in **Japan** to help bring order to that devastated nation. Now, the Army reported, **the rate of Venereal Disease among the men was increasing seriously**....

The Minister for the Army commented that "despite the Press coverage, we should realise that **VD was not invented by Australian soldiers** nor that it is peculiar to Japan." He pointed out that nothing **additional** could be done at present to reduce the high incidence.

"**Free medicine**" was the hope of the Federal Government as it **introduced its new scheme on June 1st**. **A selected range of medicines** would be offered free to most Australians....

The medical profession was reluctant to accept this. It said that **doctors should be free to decide** which drugs would be effective, and their prescriptions included drugs **other than the ones nominated by the Government**. By June 1st, **only two per cent** of doctors had signed up for the scheme. **A big battle clearly lies ahead.**

The British Empire, before the war, spanned over 30 per cent of the world's territories. A map of the world **showed the Empire in pink, and visually it looked massive.** But during the war, many of these territories asked why they were fighting for the Brits, and developed **nationalist movements that sought to escape British Rule**....

India and Israel were right now gaining such freedoms, and so-called "**armed rebellions or terrorists or** guerilla forces" were pressing the cause in dozens of other nations.

Robert Menzies was getting a message. "I can hardly imagine **a worse fate than the Empire breaking up....** Yet we could, by joint effort, come back with **as much power and influence as at any time in our history.**" **Sadly for Menzies, this did not happen**, and the Empire dwindled quickly into a shadow of its former self.

One consequence of the war was that **home deliveries of meat, and groceries and vegetables had ceased**. Now the Government was introducing legislation that would **force sellers of these goods to offer home deliveries again**. This would mean that all **the cart-pulling horses would get their jobs back**, and that horse drinking-troughs would line the streets again. Though it was too late for most of the horses. **They had long ago been sent to the vast green paddock in the sky.**

That reminds me of *Old Shep*. This was **a sad song** about a faithful old dog who eventually died. The song was initially made popular by American Red Folie, and it was the song that Elvis Presley sang as an 11-year-old to win his first prize for singing....

It was very popular in Australia in the years around 1948. No concert in the local hall in a country town on a Saturday night was complete until the local yodler with a banjo closed out the night with the lines **"but if dogs have a heaven, there's one thing I know, Old Shep has a wonderful home."**

PRICE CONTROLS END

So now I have painted a picture of a nation getting more and more annoyed with the rules and regulations that were foisted on to them by a Labor Government that still had the vision of war-time efficiences in its mind. Surely, **it thought**, it was obvious that this system of control and parsimony should be kept going, even extended, so this nation could show the world what a moderate but socialised world state could do if it tried.

So, that same Government tried an experiment that failed. Not only that, it failed so badly, and had such consequences, that **it laid the foundation for its defeat at the next elections two years hence**.

The sad story had its origin in **a war-time prices agreement** that the States had with the Federal Government in Canberra. This said that the States would give up their moderate controls **over prices** in favour of the Feds for the duration of the war, and a few years beyond. This agreement was about to expire, and it might have been hoped that a new one would replace it.

It was obvious that the process of doing this would generate a large amount of superfluous cackle. The Feds also could see that t**he States would want to go their own separate ways** and as a consequence, Canberra would surrender any chance of introducing the socialist nation they so much wanted.

Thus, they took the bold step of saying **they would hold a national referendum that gave the Government power to maintain the existing system indefinitely** and, on top of that, add even more controls.

This was a proposal that really stirred the population. People were prepared to accept the status quo, though there were growing complaints. They knew, they thought, that in due course the restraints would be removed, and business would get back to normal. But now, confronted with the possibility that these interventions would go on indefinitely, they reacted with great hostility.

The Labor Party had proposed that a referendum be held on the matter on May 29th. **Specifically**, it was to get the States to give up permanently their rights to **manage prices,** in favour of the Federal Government. But it was also seen as the thin edge of the wedge, and that soon controls would spread **so that all areas of life would be regulated**.

Response from the public was immediate and strong. There were questions about how wise Chifley was, and whether he would, if successful, raise prices on all sorts of things he "didn't himself use." Would prices be raised, and the extra revenue be taken by the Government, and so that in fact a new system of taxation would come surreptitiously into place? Would the socialist fanatics in Labor gradually turn the nation into a Fascist state, or a Communist state, with the supposed loss of all freedoms? Or even the right to own your own property?

Other issues were raised. What if the referendum failed? What would the States do if all the restraints were lifted? No one had really thought about that. Would they simply continue with the present system and perhaps gradually change it. Or might they go to the other extreme, and abolish controls completely. Which government would get the revenue from any sales taxes involved? It was all controversial stuff, as can be seen below. Criticism of the proposed Constitutional Amendment came thick and fast from all quarters.

Letter, Albert Ralph. Results prove that price-fixing controls were lifted from **the sale of farms and property** to enable prices to return to normal. The present basis of fixing defeats the object of the Act, i.e. to curtail inflation. On the contrary, **price controls have had the opposite effect, by establishing a pegged price** which really is a boom or an inflated price arrived at by inexperienced farm valuers.

Vendors of farms today find it difficult to sell within a reasonable time at the pegged price, the reason being that the pegged price is too high. Recent sales confirm that prices realised are pegged prices or under, and **some** sales considerably under. Therefore, pegged price has now become ceiling price, and control is supporting an artificial value as normal times approach.

I refer to farms as such, and not residences with a few acres, close to transport, and city houses. These command a higher price due to the housing shortage.

Comment. I enclosed this Letter not because of its clarity, but to point out that "prices" cover all aspects of any trading. Not just tea and marmalade and petrol. Every commercial transaction between all persons could be controlled by Government.

And look at the above Letter. Look at the mental conniptions that buyers and sellers were going through in the simple selling of a block of land. The newspapers were full of such Letters asking the Government to get out of the way.

Letters, Rob White, Liberal Party. Mr Chifley reeled off a formidable series of statistics showing how **prices have rocketed in the US since the abandonment**

of controls over prices. He conveniently omitted to indicate how wages there have risen correspondingly and, in fact, by comparing the real wage of the American wage-earner with those of the Australian, it is seen that the former has a great deal more advantage.

Nowhere did Chifley say that the only way to combat inflation was more production. He inclines to the belief that the only way to do this is by more controls. This, of course, perpetuates a vicious circle because the multiplicity of controls and regulations does anything but stimulate production.

Mr Chifley's bogey of Depression is likely to come about because of **the lack of incentive to produce in the atmosphere of regulation**. While production effort remains as it is, prices will remain high.

His statement that a "YES" vote would not advance Labor's platform at all will not deceive even the credulous voter. It is too widely known that control over prices and rents is an integral part of Labor's avowed plan to socialise this country.

Letters, J Liddell. During recent months, I have been making enquiries about the purchase of a second-hand car, and I am therefore happy to tell you that the cost of a good used car is less than it was six months ago, by a very considerable amount.

The trouble is that a car in good condition **can still not be purchased excepting at well above the pegged price**. I have discussed the question with a number of dealers, and without exception they attribute the situation to the steady release of new cars and, in particular, to the large numbers of English cars now or soon to be available, and their prices are too high..

This seems to point a moral. Can it be that our Canberra theorists are on too high a plane among the clouds of unreality, and that the cure for our present difficulties is not more and better controls but, in fact, **a more plentiful supply of goods and services**, and the reintroduction of competition?

As the referendum approached, the various politicians started raising their voices, both Liberal and Labour. Remember that in those days, politicians used to stump round the country delivering speeches, mainly to their own avowed converts, **in town halls, and big hotels, and public parks**. But a number of critics always managed to get in, and they were always ready to show their sophistication and good sense by jeering and catcalling, and generally managing to get ejected. It was good clean fun, but that unfortunately has now been replaced by The Box.

Ben Chifley, Prime Minister, Sydney Town Hall. Press report. Cries of "Good on yer, Ben", and "Go for yer life son" greeted Mr Chifley as he walked to the microphone last night.

During a 70-minute talk, he said that there was no suggestion by anyone, even the Liberals, that the fixing of prices and rents would be abolished. The choice now was between keeping present controls, which had held back inflation, and chaos because the States would be unable to secure uniformity. The issue was also whether controls should be exercised by the Commonwealth, which had the staff, machinery, and the experience, or by the States, which had none of these.

He warned that in the years ahead, because of factors beyond our control, many goods in this country would remain scarce. (This was seized upon by the Liberals as a warning that he would use his new powers to raise prices). He went on to say that if the States got the power, they would all bring in their own controls, and thus prices would not be uniform across the nation. (Many observers asked if this would be a bad thing). He ended by claiming that the idea that Labor wanted to take power from the States was "fantastic."

Robert Menzies, Leader of the Opposition replied to Chifley's speech. He said that it was a clever speech, and that some of his arguments were extremely attractive "like the sticky stuff on a sheet of tanglefoot."

Mr Chifley had said that if the Commonwealth abandoned its various subsidies on things like tea and butter and potatoes, the prices would skyrocket. Mr Menzies said "this is a piece of arrant blackmail of the Australian voter. At present, money for the subsidies comes specifically from the States, and if the Commonwealth stopped paying them, the States would then pay them themselves." He went on to say that it was just a big grab for power by the Labor Party, and "their Communist mates."

Comment. Menzies never missed a chance to tar Labor with the Red brush.

Arthur Fadden, Menzies' deputy leader, was very damaging in his reply. He said that when the States had pricing power **before the War**, there were no shortages, no black-markets, no queues, no ration books, and no coupons. "**When the War came**, some Canberra genius worked out **the price of 376 different brands of bird seed** and compelled every grocer who dealt in that commodity to be conversant with them. Fish merchants complain that before they can sell a pound of prawns, they have to weigh them, count them and then consult a chart which gives no less than 10 different prices for metropolitan areas, and a few extra ones for country areas.

"Prices Regulations Order No. 2416 defines an egg **as being of first quality** if it is clean, uncracked, free from stain, not thin or mis-shaped, free from blood spots (inside), with faintly visible yolk when candled, with the white translucent and firm, and with an air cell slightly tremulous and a quarter of an inch in depth. Even the humble trombone is not forgotten, as it has been the subject of four different Orders in the past year. Such a complex system cannot operate without great expense and waste."

Press report. "An interesting little competition on the hustings developed on the last night before the referendum, in Sydney's Taylor Square. A Labor Senator, Donald Grant, campaigning for a "Yes" vote, **set up his microphones** opposite Mr A Bridges, a Liberal MLC, who was supporting "No."

"Both meetings started at 8pm, so that in no time a shouting match developed. For forty-five minutes, each speaker tried to drown out the other, with the result that neither could be understood. Finally, Mr Bridges gave up, and left it all to Senator Grant, who managed another 30 minutes of harangue. A second speaker in Grant's retinue was the ubiquitous Eddie Ward, the Member for East Sydney, who made the interesting comment that he was sorry that the vote tomorrow was only to give the Commonwealth more power. He would have preferred to see it as a vote on the complete abolition of all State parliaments."

In the last few weeks, both sides pulled out all stops, and the newspaper adverts proliferated. Women's groups, too, got involved. For example, the Women's Movement Against Socialism placed adverts they could ill afford in the Sydney papers, and ended with financial difficulties. A different group, the New Housewives Association, held successful rallies against higher prices in Sydney streets. Both show **a level of political activism among women that had been virtually absent since the War.**

On Saturday, May 29, the people voted. The result was a resounding defeat for the government, and the final result was a "No" vote of about 60 per cent. Given that the number of voters then who always voted for their **inherited** political party, the vote of 40 percent for the Government was a real slap in the face. It said that the people were heartily sick of price fixing and all controls, and they wanted change.

LABOR'S REACTION

Chifley and the Labor Party had not expected to lose the referendum by such a large margin, and the loss came as a crushing blow to many of them. Of course, it is an Australian tradition to knock back referendum proposals, especially those that give more power to the Feds. But, having said that, Labor had won the elections eighteen months earlier quite easily, and it seemed that nothing major had happened to change opinions. So the first reaction was surprise or shock. This was accompanied by the feeling, among the Left wing of the Party, that this was no good at all for their dreams of socialising this nation. In all, it was a bitter disappointment.

The State Governments were instantly deluged with good advice.

Letters, E Spooner. The people have expressed themselves clearly, and the Federal Government hastens to evacuate certain fields of control. This is a convenient stage to re-examine the beliefs some of us have expressed in recent years.

The defeat of the referendum is not necessarily a mandate for the exercise of prices control by the States. In my view, a return to the natural condition is the surest way to a safe recovery, and I believe that to be a correct interpretation of the public verdict.

The establishment of **a new set of State prices controls will create more difficulties for the future**. It will be extraordinary if six State governments of various political shades **can agree to and ensure the passage** through their Parliaments of legislation sufficiently uniform for a prices control scheme to function throughout Australia. Even if that miracle were to happen, constitutional infringements may keep the law courts very busy.

The proper course for the Federal Government is to **ease controls gradually during the next seven months**, and allow the present legislation to lapse at December 31. If the States desire to resume rental controls at that stage, this would be practicable, although I am convinced that those States that leave well alone will more quickly solve their housing problems and arrive at fair rentals.

If we believe that the elimination of controls will stimulate production, and that prices and charges will find their level by the restoration of competition, this is the time to say so, and to urge that policy. Why create **a new vested interest in State bureaucracy to continue the mischievous interference with enterprise and production commenced by the doomed Federal men?**

If the transition from experimental socialism to healthy enterprise involves some short period of chaos, let us act quickly to get a national foundation upon which our national economy can be reconstructed.

We may be surprised to find out how very short a transitional period turns out to be, and I fully expect that the longer the present controls are continued, the greater will be the difficulties in their eventual eradication.

But Mr Spooner could not be allowed to get away unscathed with that.

Letters, J Bensted. Mr Spooner's letter says, in effect, that the States will not be able to carry out prices control, and advances cogent argument in support of this view.

This is, of course, a distinct contradiction of one of the main arguments for the "NO" vote. Before the vote was taken, we were told that the States could, and would, give more effective control. Now we are told that the States cannot do it at all.

Apparently Mr Spooner has revealed the true attitude of at least an influential section of the "NO" campaign. That is, they want no control by either Canberra or the States, and an open go by everyone. To use a bit of slang, these "NO" advocates sold the people a pup.

In the next month, pup or no pup, **the Government reacted with a series of important measures**. It first of all sulked a bit, and said that there was no way that the States could **manage** price controls, and repeated its mantra that the nation would end up with potatoes at one price in Melbourne, and a different price in Perth. But sanity quickly prevailed, and Chifley swung round and got ahead of the clock. In mid-June, he announced that the Federal Government would **relinquish administration of rent control** in two months, and of **price fixing of land sales** in four months. And he announced that he would move out of **all other controls by December 31, or earlier**.

Chifley went on to declare the withdrawal from providing **subsidies** on goods such as tea, butter and cheese, potatoes, raw cotton, goat skins and pickled pelts, and a dozen other products. The idea of these subsidies had been to help the consumer pay for them, via the magnanimity of the Federal Government, though the money in most cases came directly from the States. There is no doubt that they helped to keep prices down, though on the other side they helped to keep taxes up. Anyway, within a few months, they were due to be scrapped, and this posed problems for the States. Would they too scrap them, or would they continue them? It was a decision each State had to make on its own. I will return to these questions later.

But Chifley was not yet finished. Clothes production had increased to the point where there were plenty of clothes to go round, yet not enough coupons to buy them. Where do you think they went? Onto the black market, because **there you only needed money to buy**. This was a system that was clearly doomed in the face of vastly increasing production.

So, Chifley dropped another bombshell. He announced that **rationing of meat and clothing would "end tomorrow"**. This came as a surprise to most people, even though, for example, the clothes industry had been campaigning for it for months. After about eight years, all of those coupons were now useless, and could be thrown away or burnt. Almost everyone welcomed this move. Mrs Eleanor Glencross, of the Housewives Association, said "all women will welcome the news. Clothes rationing has outlived its usefulness. Butchers will be relieved of all coupon worries when they start to deliver meat." Mr

Buckingham, of the Retail Traders' Association said cryptically "The Prime Minister has acted wisely and well."

A few people expressed fear that would be a stampede for these goods. Also, that prices would rise, and that there would not be enough of them to go round. But such was not the case.

The next day, the only increase in trading was seen in a demand for linen and Manchester goods, and towels. In this case, retail stores reported that they were able to provide, for example, four pairs of sheets to each customer, with the promise of more to come when they re-filled their inventories in a day or two. Other items of clothing saw no increase in demand, and meat orders remained at the previous levels. The sky did not fall in.

The main dislocation from Chifley's last announcement was in Canberra where **over a thousand persons were out of work immediately**, because their jobs went away at the same time as rationing did. Most of these were "transferred" to other Departments, and others were absorbed by private enterprise, which was short of good people at this time. There was a similar job fall-out in the States. For example, 600 clerks employed by the retail trade to check clothing coupons were thrown out of work.

All of this **handed the States a big, fat, can of worms**. Each of them now had to decide what they would put into place to substitute for the Commonwealth withdrawal. The Commonwealth was salaciously saying that it would be a complete mess, and that the States would end up with different prices all over the place, and that their existing system controls were the only way to go. "Don't say we didn't warn you", was their attitude.

The first reaction of the States was to simply copy the Federal regulations without change, for an immediate stand-by. But at a Conference in June, the Premiers met and started to work closely together to avoid the threatening chaos. They **resolved to remove as many controls as possible**, and to retain only those where it could be argued that they were still needed, on key commodities and services.

So successful were they, that all States together, on September 20, announced **that 50,000 items would henceforth be exempt from price controls**. Needless to say, this is a huge number, and it was promised that the remaining 20,000 items were being reviewed at a rapid rate. **So the time-bomb that the Federal government left for the States was unexploded**, and a major improvement in the lives of ordinary people was achieved. It is interesting to speculate on how much unnecessary trouble those restraints had caused before they were abolished.

Summary. The prices referendum was to me a most significant point in Australian history. Prior to that date, the Labor Party had been quietly following Britain's lead on socialism. The Brits had recently nationalised the coal mines, and the health industry, and were talking tough about other industries. There can be no doubt that Chifley was headed the same way. He liked the idea of rationing and controls, he wanted the nationalisation of the banks, and control of wages and rents and the prices of most things. In fact, he wanted a planned economy, half way to

Communism, but without all the rigours that that would bring.

So he went to the people to get the power to perpetuate Commonwealth controls over prices, and rents, and wages. **The people knocked him back in no uncertain terms.** They did not want these things. To his credit, he soon realised this, and that is where the spate of announcements I have just described came from. That is, from **the realisation that the socialisation of Australia was not a political possibility**. Of course, such a realisation did not come to all Labor figures at the same time, and many continued with the theme for a few years. And, the whole idea was not dead until the Courts later threw out his proposed nationalisation of the banks. But, with this referendum came that first realisation that **his plans for the great Australian socialist state were not going to come to fruition, and that he had better acknowledge that quickly**.

NEW TECHNOLOGIES

New Light Wool Fabric: A report from ICI, London, indicated that a new form of ultra-light wool has been designed in the UK. It promised to "revolutionise the whole field of lightweight and tropical clothing". It was composed of 95% wool with 5% of nylon, and made to be extra strong.

This was the very beginning of the vast changes that swept the textile industry from that time. Within a very few years, clothing that was 100 per cent nylon was everywhere, and the old fabrics, such as wool, were well and truly on the downward path.

Some of you will remember Alec Guinness in a 1951 British movie called *The Man in the White Suit.* In that movie, he invented a nylon fabric that he hoped would last forever, and would be of immense benefit to the world. Alas, his plans were foiled by the bad industrialists who worried about the steady flow of their profits. At this time, the phrase "planned obsolescence" came into being. Of course, most things we buy nowadays have this type of planning built in. How often does something fail just after the warranty runs out? I think adding this type of sophistication to the engineering process is a stroke of genius – for the manufacturer.

Washing machines, when they came on the scene, changed Mondays forever. Remember those steamy laundries, with the fire beneath a copper full of boiling water, and the scrubbing board and hand wringer poised at the ready. What a lot of fun it was to keep the fuel up to the fire; how great it was to lift the boiling clothes out of the copper with the stick, and get face-fulls of steam and spray up your arms and into your shoes. Oh yes, it was a lot of fun. What a pity the good old days are going.

Flies Resisting DDT: Researchers in Florida, on behalf of the US Department of Agriculture, discovered that flies were becoming increasingly resistant to DDT. They said that with each successive generation of flies, the poison would have less effect.

Here, there was no suggestion at this time that DDT's effects were diminishing, and absolutely no suggestion that it was a killer of humans. That took a long time to filter through to the entire world, because DDT was so very effective against both weeds and insects in many ways. In Australia, opposition to its use only took off round 1980.

BREACH OF PROMISE

Mr Tom Right was awarded Ten Pounds today for breach of promise. Judge Markell said the suit was quite different from any other he had heard, because this time the plaintiff was a man.

The lady involved was a Miss Hampton, and she had initially proposed that they go to a registry office to get married right away. However, they agreed that they should wait a while and do it properly. They decided to marry after Tom had spent some time working in his job in Crookwell, while she was in Sydney.

He had given her ten Pounds to buy a wedding dress. When he came to Sydney, she had told him she was finished and would not marry him. She refused to return his ten Pounds, and simply said she had changed her mind. Mr Right said he was deeply hurt by her refusal. He had claimed four hundred Pounds from the lady. The judge consoled him by telling him that all marriages were a lottery

JULY NEWS ITEMS

News Item, *SMH* front page. An opossum entered a house in Sydney's Strathfield and **gave birth to twins in a laundry basket**. Front page news indeed!

The Federal Government will soon call for tenders to **build six television broadcasting units** that will service the six State Capitals. At the moment, there is no suggestion that commercial stations will be allowed....

In fact, **TV did not arrive Australia until 1956**, a day prior to the opening of the Olympic Games in Melbourne. **Sydney and Melbourne** were the only cities covered and, as well as the **ABC**, each of these cities had **two commercial broadcasters**.

"Sources close to the trade" are alarmed that there will **not be enough flags and bunting available** in Australia to ensure **appropriate decorations for the Royal Tour of Australia next year**. It is not yet clear who will come, or when, but a Royal Tour is certain....

Australia's shortage of US dollars will impede imports of cloth. Also, current stockpiles were sold in the Army Disposal sales after the War. It is expected that English woollen bunting, and calico made in China, might help fill the gap, but **local manufacturers will be forced to use inferior materials. In any case, a national bunting crisis is looming.**

The basic wage varies between States, and the current weekly pay is about 6 Pounds. But workers in isolated **Broken Hill have a basic wage of 17 Pounds.** To get this, workers must be **members of an appropriate**

Union, and have been born and educated in Broken Hill, or have lived there for seven years....

This disparity in pay rates is causing friction, but the general attitude there is that if you don't like it, **then go away.** And **the envy from all workers outside the Silver City** is a wonder to behold.

The NSW **Minister for Education visited a primary school** at Sydney's Kogarah. After inspecting the school, he gave it **a half-holiday, effective immediately**. The children cheered wildly. This **was the custom at the time** whenever a Minister visited a school....

That would never do in these more modern times. Teachers would complain that their planned lessons could not be delivered, **mothers would despair** because their routine of pick-up was disrupted. And because **the children would be left wandering** the streets till Mum came home from work....

Times **have** changed.

The Chairman of the London-based **British Empire Cancer Campaign** was pleased with **the results of trials using two new drugs**. He said "these are the first instances of control of cancer without using surgery or rays. It appears that **the secrets of the cancer cell,** and the way in which it develops, **will no longer elude us.**"

Comment. Sadly, **the search for keys to these secrets** has continued on for many years, and despite some considerable progress, **is still elusive in many cases.**

If you fired kunny-knuckle, what sport would you be playing?

WHITE AUSTRALIA POLICY

Prior to the War, and during it, a number of Asians, such as Indonesians and Malays, had come illegally to Australia and had remained here without detection. By 1948, the Federal Government was tracking these people down, and deporting them in batches of a dozen or so every few weeks. The numbers involved were quite small, and they had no political friends, so their departure went almost unnoticed. The vast majority of Australians thought that because they were here illegally, they had no right to stay. And of course, **they were Asians as well**. Some of the deportees had married Australian girls, and were the fathers of Australian children. For example, in March, the deportation of a particular Malay was delayed four months, so that he could wait here for the birth of his fifth child. So, this expression of the White Australia Policy went on quietly in the background, with hardly any fuss.

This attitude to Asians was very widespread in the community. Most people in Australia had no particular animosity to most Asians, other than the Japanese. They just thought that we here should preserve our British heritage, and only dilute it with some good stock from Europe. Like the Greeks and Italians. And later, perhaps "the Poles and Balts." And this attitude was scarcely challenged, because our immigration policy simply excluded the entry of Asians, from whatever country. This was the status quo, and it seemed it would remain fully status.

But later in 1948, some cracks started to appear in this impassable wall. They came about because Australian soldiers had gone to Japan as a peace-keeping force, and, spurred on by a series of edicts prohibiting fraternisation with the local girls, had ended up the proud fathers of little Eurasian bundles of joy. Our Government, under the paternal leadership of Chifley and Calwell, said that this was too bad, and that **under no circumstance could the Japanese families come and live in Australia** when the soldiers returned from their tour of duty.

This started a small controversy. It is important to remember that at this time we were just three years from the end of the War in which Japan had tried to invade Australia, and had killed and captured and tortured hundreds of thousands of our soldiers. **Resentment and hatred of all things Japanese was still extremely strong**. So what we now had was a battle in the Letters columns, between those who wanted to have nothing to do with the Japanese, and those who thought less violently towards them.

I enclose some of this correspondence below. To me, it is interesting because here, for the first time, we have some people advocating a more moderate line towards the Japanese. Let me add that such a line was by no means typical of Australians as a whole, because for years the dislike remained the dominant attitude. But this little glimmer of forgiveness that was then shown was significant in the larger picture we now see, 70 years later, that the Japanese are considered by most as good and as trustworthy as neighbours can be.

In March, Arthur Calwell, then the Minister for Immigration, had refused an application by an Australian soldier for his Japanese wife to enter this country. The reason given was quite straightforward, in that it was against the White Australia Policy. The response to this was immediate.

Letters, Mary Jackson. Mr Calwell's latest edict, that no Australian who marries a Japanese may bring him or her into Australia, smacks of the superior race doctrine, a feature of the ideologies against which the war was fought.

Mr Calwell does not say how it is that he knows better than his fellow Australians whom is fit and proper for the latter to marry. His assumption that all Japanese are to be lumped together and condemned outright is as stupid as it would be to suggest that, because we are both Australians, Mr Calwell and I are similar in all respects.

Letters, R Burford. Apart from the right of every man to choose his own wife, I would like to remind Mr Calwell that our nation is supposed to be Christian, and that the lowly Nazarene came to tell us that in the sight of God, there are no racial barriers.

He also taught us to **forgive our enemies**, and the sooner we, individually and as a nation, attempt to follow Him, the sooner a true and lasting peace will settle on this world.

Letters, Frank Everingham. Clearly the young man in Japan was ill advised in what he did. But that aside, Calwell's decision is a direct challenge to the fundamental rights of a free British citizen. The marriage of a male British subject to any foreign national has always, subject to quarantine regulations and security vetting, been a passport to Australia, and recognised as part of British liberties and freedoms. Note too that his parents are prepared to accept her and their grandchild.

Letters, M Warren Secretary, Aust. Board of Missions. Those of us, who have recently been in

Japan, know that Mr Calwell's insult to every Japanese will do more harm than good. His virulence will be published widely in Japan to the embarrassment of our men and the ultimate hurt of our country.

Letters, C Pilcher, Diocesan Church House. In sending our men to Japan upon their service to our country, we are placing them in a position in which some relationship with the opposite sex is almost inevitable. Then we cry out at them "such relationships must be illegal, you are not allowed to marry."

The refusal of the Government seems to be based upon the idea that no Japanese can be a worthy human being. I need hardly point out that excellent people can be found in every nation, as well as those who are less excellent. Burke, one of the wisest statesmen of the 18th century, said "it is impossible to bring an indictment against a whole nation." Apparently, our leaders are not as wise as Burke.

Letters, E Huxtable. If Mr Calwell's ban had been restricted to marriage in a Shinto temple, then it would have been understood. But he applies his ruling to marriage in a Christian church, and to any child of such a marriage.

Even if the first case is not a renunciation of the Christian ethic, the second certainly is so. So also is the violence, bitterness, and extravagance of his language. His sentiments will not bring consolation to the war-bereaved, but will tend towards the opposite.

Letters, J Yorke. Mr Calwell's action in banning the Japanese wives smacks of maudlin sentimentalism. **If he is seriously worried about the feelings of wives and mothers** of Australian servicemen "being outraged" by the entry of ex-enemy nationals, it is a wonder he has not banned German and Italian migrants.

Basic socialist philosophy does not support Calwell's action. Socialism must oppose racial and cultural barriers such as we have in Australia. For the sake of international goodwill, all our governments must rid themselves of this long tradition of racial and cultural exclusiveness.

Comment. The above Letters are a sample from a larger pool that were opposed to Calwell, and were often based on Christianity and ethics. This is often the case with Letters, and it continues right through till today. The next set of Letters is quite different, and centre on the bitterness that people had about the Japanese.

Letters, Mary Wall. I do hope you will allow my small **paeon of praise for the stand taken by the Minister**, and his very definite ruling. The article published lately in one of our newspapers of an Australian soldier, having so little decency that he stood up in a Shinto temple before a heathen idol to go through a form of marriage, must shock all right-minded Australians and fill them with great misgiving.

Letters, Anna O'Donoughue. I express my thanks and admiration to our outspoken and fearless Mr Calwell. Too many people are willing to whitewash our late (and, I argue, present) enemies, the Japanese.

Let the Japanese stay in their own country, and let Australians live in happiness in theirs – the land for which so many gallant sailors, soldiers, and airmen died, not forgetting the murdered nurses and civilians.

Letters, B Moriarty. I am amazed at the apathetic reaction to the suggestion that certain Japanese be granted Australian nationality. Do the comfortable advocates of freedom, brotherly love, and toleration seriously suggest that **such blood be permitted to taint future generations of Australians**? To allow this would be a criminal betrayal of our brothers who suffered martyrdom to save Australia. Such freedom that we enjoy was won in agony, and should not be surrendered to queasy sentimentality.

Letters, Louis Samuels. One would think that 99 per cent of Australian soldiers would think very hard before taking the fatal step of marrying a Japanese girl.

It is a little too early to be influenced by the Christian attitude to one's enemies, and if these cruel-minded Orientals can sufficiently convince the democracies in the years to come that they are really in search of peace, even then much care will have to be exercised.

Those people who oppose Mr Calwell in this matter take little account of the effort required to keep the Japanese from invading these shores, and can have little imagination as what the consequences of failure would have been.

Letters, G Hunty. May I, as the mother of a beloved boy who lies buried somewhere in Burma, express my deep admiration of Mr Calwell for the stand he has taken. No decent Australian could bear to allow Japanese into this country that our men suffered and died for.

The World Council of Churches, Australian Division, weighed in at this point. It described the Policy as a constant irritant to other races. It went on to say that the exclusion of other races was justified by arguments that cited the maintenance of living standards, the unity of culture, and the requirements of defence. But, said the Council, all of these can be gained by means other than exclusion. Whatever our justification in the past, it was no longer relevant.

Finally, I close with two comments on the WCC position. Here again, the vote is split. On the one hand a tentative welcome to people regardless of their colour, and on the other, a straight-out colour antipathy.

Letters, Kerwin Maegreath. The timely statement issued by the Australian section of the WCC should find widespread support. That our Policy gives offence to the teeming millions of coloured neighbours in the Pacific goes without saying. The men of the Second AIF remember well that at El Alamein, black Indian soldiers fought nobly on our side against such enemies as the Italians, who kicked us in the back when they thought the Allies were down, and by whose hands thousands of Australians fell in battle.

In World War II, Indian soldiers won 40 Victoria Crosses. Yet, **none of these men are admitted to this open-space continent on even the barest quota system, preference being given to former enemies, like Italians.**

After all, most of these so-called "coloured" people are no darker than a Bondi lifesaver. If they can help develop our rural areas, why not let them.

Letters, Donald Clarke. I cannot agree with the WCC. There are certain races who are, without a doubt, inferior in many ways to our standard of life, and it would be a mistake to permit such peoples to add to our present difficulties in attempting to lift Australia culturally to a higher place in world eyes. I feel sure that we can retain the love of mankind of another colour, and show true friendliness in many ways to other countries, but at the same time prosecute our present White Australia Policy.

Comment. The opinions show a mixed bag of ideas, some **for** the Asians, and some **against**. Overall, they do show a glimmer of forgiveness towards the Japanese, but obviously this nation still had a long way to go in this. And beyond that, beyond the Japanese, there was still quite a bit of opposition to Asians in general. The colour of their skin remained a big influence on Policy.

Finally, the last word from the Ministry for Immigration, July 22. The Minister, Mr Arthur Calwell, **is opposed to a quota** for the admission of Asian migrants, similar to that of America. This would allow a maximum of **five persons from any Asiatic country to enter Australia each year**.

He is of the opinion that once the door to Australia was opened for permanent residence of a small number of Asians, continued pressure would be exerted to permit larger numbers to reside permanently in this country. It is clear that Asiatic countries would like to send large numbers here.

"Entry of such people could have only one end. That is, the complete abandonment of our present policy and the opening wide of our gates to many races of people who vastly outnumber us and whose manners of life, religious beliefs, and culture, differ widely from ours. The end result would **be the conquest of Australia by infiltration, as surely as by direct assault**."

Comment. This statement by Calwell shows how deep his feelings were against Asians. It is hard to imagine **now,** as we walk around our cities, that such paranoia existed against **all** Asians. There is no doubt that the hatred towards Japanese was there, but against all other Asians? No, I do not think so.

To me, Calwell was a long way out of touch with public opinion in saying that we could not admit five Singaporeans or Indians, say, a year. Our soldiers had fought shoulder to shoulder with these same people, and as some of the above Letters show, there were many who would have been happy to allow some small quota, and take the risk of these five or more people blossoming into the conquest by infiltration that Calwell said he feared.

NEWS AND VIEWS

New Art Teaching: Traditionally, in Art classes for primary school students, pupils drew everything (apart from the notorious gumleaf) with the assistance of a ruler. However, in 1948 a growing number of teachers rebelled against this, encouraging students to draw "free hand" and to use their imaginations.

Saturday Burials Banned: In the spate of industrial and union actions during 1948, it was decided that burials on Saturdays would now be banned. This was a result of a decision by the Undertakers' Assistants and Cemetery Employees' Union, who resolved to only work from Monday to Friday in the future. The decision is expected to cause major difficulties.

Letters, Mick Datson, Broken Hill. All people must agree that dress reform for men in hot weather is long overdue, and I think it is because the right people are not taking the lead. Perhaps one or more of our important schools could start the ball rolling by instituting a cool uniform of shorts and blouses for students. Older men will not break away from traditions, while young lads are still wearing the neck-to-knee rigout. Do we ever stop to consider how ridiculous we dress compared to what the average female wears?

Comment. Office wear for men remains as stuffy as ever in cities. School gear has improved a lot. Recreation clothes now include a new uniform that revolves round blue jeans. And that includes females. Ugh.

Surf Club Escorts: Members of the Maroubra Surf Club escorted five women to their homes last night. The women were returning home after a dance at the Coogee Surf Club. Following the spate of violence that had broken out in the preceding days, the members of the Club offered to escort the women to their homes. Coogee lifesavers would be available from next week to protect women returning home late at night. The Club telephone number for bookings is FX 4538.

Flirtation as Preparation for Marriage: British Doctor, Marjorie Tait, believes flirtation to be excellent preparation for marriage. She has reported that if young people are deprived of flirtation opportunities, they committed themselves too early in their lives.

Australians Emotionally Unstable: The Bishop of Armidale, Dr Moyes, created waves when he claimed that Australians were emotionally unstable and could not discuss ideas rationally. He said that our education has not succeeded in its task of creating in its students an emotional stability, a mental flexibility and a spirit of adventure.

He went on to say that a slump in the nation's morals had accompanied the falling off of church attendances.

Roman Catholic objection: In England, Cardinal Griffin reacted strongly in opposition to statements made by the

Lord Chancellor, Lord Jowitt. Jowitt declared that marriage was not necessarily for the procreation of children, nor was procreation of children the principal end of marriage. Cardinal Griffin, however, informed the Catholic Parents Association that contraceptive intercourse, with or without the aid of instruments, was not true consummation of marriage. This has remained one of the foremost teachings of the Catholic Church, and is one that has been behind a great deal of discontent within the rank and file of practising Catholics for over half a century.

No First Prize for writing competition: In late 1947, the Sydney Morning Herald ran a Short Story Contest. The results were decided in 1948, and were a shock to all people who participated. The judges decided that none of the literature entered was of a sufficient standard to deserve the first prize. A second prize, however, was awarded.

The rabbit trade was quite large, before the days when myxomatosis decimated rabbit numbers across the nation. Here is a letter that talks about its role in the nation's economy.

Letters, Jim Rickwood. In view of the serious dollar position, it is difficult to understand the action of the Federal Government in repeatedly imposing the 1/6 levy on every pound of rabbit skins exported. The Minister for Commerce, Mr Pollard, is reported to have said that most of the rabbit skins marketed in Australia were exported to America, and were second only to wool as a dollar earner.

Yet, repeatedly, when skins have been at their best and trappers have been destroying large numbers of the worst pest with which the landowner has to contend, the Government has imposed its export levy and invariably caused a collapse of the market. The levy has recently been suspended, but, according to the press reports, only until April 30 next. This is ridiculous, for it is not until then that skins become of marketable value. No Government responsible for the imposition of this levy can claim to be acting in Australia's best interests.

At the time, eating of rabbits was not just restricted to rabbit stew. There were dozens of recipes that floated through the columns of ladies' readings. Here is one, for potted rabbit, that you might like to try yourself.

It is taken from the Weston Presbyterian Ladies Recipe Book of 1948.

Potted Rabbit

Boil a rabbit until the flesh falls off the bone. Throw away the bones. Take the flesh, and put it through a fine mincer. Add the secret herbs that your mother entrusted only to her most handsome son. Mix thoroughly. Put out into bowls that have been well washed if they have been used for sanitary purposes overnight. Allow to cool for 12 hours in a refrigerator. Eat thinly sliced on toast. If you re-heat it too much, you might get a form of food poisoning that is often quite mild.

AUGUST NEWS ITEMS

A baby giraffe, born a few days ago at Sydney's Taronga Park Zoo, is **growing at the rate of two inches per day**. She is now **six feet, six inches tall**, and is "all neck and legs and looking beautiful".

Ex-Servicemen are to get special treatment in some cases. For example, if **any ordinary citizen** owns a rental property he **must give 18 months notice to a tenant to quit**. But new rules say that an ex-Serviceman owner must give only **six months notice**....

In a second example, if the ordinary citizen owner **lets a property to a tenant and that is sub-let**, the owner can evict both people only if he can **find them both** suitable accommodation in exchange. But now, for the ex-Servicemen owner, he needs to find alternative accommodation **only for the tenant, and not for the sub-letter**....

The wonder of this is not so much the special consideration given to ex-Servicemen, but instead the maze of hoops that all classes were **forced to jump through to remove tenants, and the time (and law cases) involved.**

In Britain, 100 medical students volunteered for a **special diet on which they consumed only food pills**. The pills contained only food concentrates, and chemicals to quench thirst. They were flavoured with peppermint, orange and coffee, **and for a Sunday treat, chop suey**....

The medical scientist who conducted the trial said it proved that **mankind can survive for six days on**

tablets carried in a coat pocket. He did not say why anyone would want to do this.

In Darwin, a medical Dr Webber, the Member for Tennant Creek, told a Government inquiry that **four bottles of beer a day was the minimum requirement for a working man in the Northern Territory**. Other people calculated that the cost of this would be almost equal to the basic wage. So presumably, **many "working men" could either eat or drink beer**.

Australia is not doing so well in the **London Olympic Games**. The Games are almost over and so far **we have no Gold medals for swimming, and only one elsewhere**. But as **our officials were quick to point out**, of course, it was not winning that counts but just **the joy to be had from merely competing**.

A 19-year-old elephant arrived by ship in Sydney on its way to Taronga Park It was a gift from London Zoo. She had remained in her crate throughout the voyage, but was placid and friendly when she was released. She **played a mouth-organ for the watching crowd**, and ate fruit by the bucket-full....

Also on board were pairs of jaguars and black rhinos, and an armadillo. There were dozens of flamingoes, and 300 brightly plumed parrots from South Africa.

Stop Press. Sculler and policeman Mervyn Woods won Gold at the Olympics. This brings the Australian total to two Golds. The other Gold was John Winter in the High Jump.

MEDICAL MATTERS

Throughout July and August, the Government announced details of its free medicine scheme. It promised that all patients in Australia would be able to get a number of drugs for free, provided they did not have too many bites at the cherry. Of course, it only covered the more commonly used drugs, and excluded the rarer and more costly ones. But the scheme was well intentioned, and was designed to make quite a difference to people's costs. It was not to cover medical care, nor hospital care, **only the cost of drug**s.

Looking back from 2018, at the various Government and private schemes available now, it seems small beer. But **then** it was a major step forward. In fact, as we shall see, it **might** have been a step so far forward that it **might** have led to socialised medicine, and that **might** mean the co-option of all doctors to be employed by the Government.

When the scheme was first announced, the *Sydney Morning Herald* reported that only two percent of doctors would support it. The support of doctors was of paramount importance, since the drugs were available only on their prescription. The British Medical Association, which was the "trade union" that Australian doctors belonged to, said it opposed the plan because the number of drugs in it was inadequate, and would force doctors to prescribe inadequate medicines, and expose them to the entreaties of patients for what they considered superior drugs. They also resented not being able to prescribe as they thought fit for patients, and the fact that they were suddenly were under the threat of penalties and discipline if they did not stick to the letter of the law.

This was the official stated position of the BMA, and it doubtless played its part. But also pertinent was the knowledge that the whole health industry in Britain had just been socialised, and **doctors en masse had become public servants**. This free medicine **here was seen as the thin edge of the wedge**, and visionaries could see our doctors being regimented here as well. The tactic that the doctors used publicly here was not to fight on any of the policy matters mentioned above, but generally on the inadequacies of **the forms** designed for prescribing treatments. This was something of a red herring, but it left the serious matters for behind-the-scenes negotiation.

A doctor from North Sydney said "we all support a good scheme, but this one is outmoded. It sets the profession back 35 years. We want to give the public something better than it now has, not something worse."

A doctor from Burwood said "the need we have today is for more hospital beds. It is useless fobbing people off with more medicine."

A doctor from Newtown said "I live in a slum area, and the crying need is for preventive medicine, not bottles of physic. If the government is serious, let it remove the slums and the squalor where TB breeds."

Letters, Douglas Stuart. The proposed scheme is certainly not prompted by concern for the health of the people of Australia. It is a clumsy political trick which has deceived nobody and no amount of amending will make it anything else. The very name is dishonest, since, even if we agree to use Commonwealth forms, the medications would not be free. All people pay for our social services, and when this free medicine is used, **the social services payments go up for all of us**.

As for benefits, this Act would only tend to increase an already deplorably high consumption of medicine and to encourage the superstition that good health can be doled out in eight ounce bottles.

The only way the BMA and Senator McKenna can save their faces is by letting this stillborn monster be buried and deservedly forgotten. Then the BMA can show him a hundred things urgently crying out for his attention, and can promise him the whole-hearted co-operation of the medical profession.

The Trade Unions had their bit to say. They wanted free medicine as proposed. They came up with all sorts of threats to the doctors such as instructing their members not to visit doctors who refused to sign up.

Letters, J Fuller. We live in an interesting age. Union officials declare that the BMA boycott on the free medicine scheme is vicious, and that doctors have no right to withhold free medicine.

Poor unionists. One immediately thinks of the many people affected by the withholding of gas supplies, the many people affected by the withholding of coal supplies, and the lack of decent transport. Also those builders affected by strikes and material shortages, and the farm lands being overrun by rabbits because of netting shortage, and so on, ad infinitum.

I, for one, am pleased the boot has changed foot. There are two sides in everything.

Letters, P Pickle. So, Mr J Healy, Federal Secretary of the Watersiders' Federation, thinks the doctors should be compelled to prescribe on the mandatory forms against their wills and better judgement.

The right to withhold their services has always been claimed by the watersiders, miners, and others, notwithstanding the effects on the community. Mr Healy, however, objects strongly when he is faced with similar action, and obviously resents having to swallow some of his own medicine, which he and others like him have for too long been so freely and willingly dishing out for thousands of others at any old time and under conditions which make such actions far less justifiable.

A few more doses of this medicine might bring Mr Healy and those who think like him to their senses and alter their "Nelson" view of strikes.

Letters, J Emdur. No doctors with any scruples expect fees from the necessitous and the indigent, and they can already obtain the best of drugs and preparations from any public hospital free of charge. I look about me and note that the most illustrious and imminent men in the profession already do the greater part of their work in public hospitals, and deem it an honour and privilege to be able to do so.

As for free medicine, I am still trying to find a patient who wants it. They would find it much cheaper to have the iniquitous social services tax abolished, and pay for medicine only as they require it.

Nobody can convince me that the incessant swallowing of medicine makes for a healthy nation. Many physicians prefer to order proprietary pills, capsules or tablets in a pleasant and convenient form, feeling that far too many mixtures go down the sink anyway.

The debate was just starting. It is still going on. We all get free medicine now, except for the stuff we have to pay for. We can get any particular medicine we want, except for the ones we can't get. Maybe we should pass laws saying that people will not get sick and need medicine.

CHIFLEY'S BANKING BILL

The Labor Party had set up legislation for a Commonwealth Bank in 1912, and since then it made some headway as a savings bank for small lenders, but it had not captured much the business from the Big End of Town. During the Depression years about 1930, Ben Chifley saw the private banks cut back drastically on their lending activities, and in particular, watched them foreclose on borrowers who could not keep up their mortgage payments.

From that point forward, **he did everything he could to thwart those banks**. As soon as he got into office he introduced two Bills to give the Treasury more control over private banks, and generally let it be known that his antipathy was destined to cause them grief.

Trouble really started a year ago in August, 1947. **And it was big trouble.** On Friday 15, the High Court rejected a Bill that Chifley had proposed **to force all Councils to bank Commonwealth**. The next day, a Saturday, Cabinet sat, and decided to **nationalise all private banks in Australia.** This meant that the private banks would be bought out by the Commonwealth Bank, and that they would cease to exist. Instead of walking down the street and seeing a bank on every second corner, the customer would see only one bank, and be forced to do business with that.

This had **not** been part of the Labor Party's pre-election platform, and it came as a complete shock. Business in general was stunned. Every private bank was knocked senseless, and legions of customers were aghast. As the

Sydney Morning Herald put it in a headline *Bank Decision Staggers Community; Millions Involved*. It went on to say that the plan had shocked the business world, and would result in the creation of an 800 million Pound monopoly. There were nine banks affected, and between them they had 2633 branches throughout Australia. At that time, they had advances totalling 649 million Pounds to the public, compared to the 22 million Pounds that the Commonwealth had advanced. **It was indeed the most outrageous takeover proposal.**

Criticism of this Bill was swift and violent, and often. I list below the main points of the diatribes directed against it.

Mr Menzies, Leader of Opposition. "This comes out of a clear sky. They have no mandate to do this. It is directly opposite from the 1936 Royal Commission findings."

T Bruxnor, Country Party Leader, NSW. "Nationalisation will kill social, and economic, and political freedom, and dampen down enterprise. It will put the yoke of totalitarianism on the neck of every Australian."

Other complaints over the months that followed talked of the government's apparent policy of crippling business enterprise; of paralysing a businessman who wanted to express opinions different from the government; of the dangers of doctrinaire Socialists who want to circumvent the peoples' will; and of the end of our cherished rights and liberties. There were innumerable other opinions, that castigated Chifley and his "henchmen."

The Sydney Herald pointed out that nationalised banking was the corner stone of Soviet Russia and allowed it to maintain its totalitarian rule. The Editorial left no doubt.

"This move is one of the most revolutionary in the history of the country. Yet the Prime Minister, with casual or contemptuous concern for the opinions of the public, contents himself with a curt announcement of Cabinet's decision, without condescending one word to justify or explain it."

Supporters of the Bill argued that commercial banks were heartless, and they denied loans to the working class and gave them to big business. They also drew on a well-spring of resistance in pointing to foreclosures on homes during the Depression. Further, they argued with justification, that having so many banks was inefficient, and the nine banks were just duplicating services. They had some good points, but all the means of communicating with the people in general were controlled by those who opposed the legislation, so the **supporters of the Bill were not much heard**. But there were hundreds of Letters that were heard, and I publish just two to give you a feel for them.

Letters, D Campbell. It is difficult to find any other reason for the Bill other than the desire to nationalise. And not just the Banks, but everything and every aspect of our society. You notice that a couple of years ago, the Labor Party tried to nationalise the airlines. And a few months ago, they took-over half of Qantas, so that the government now owns all of that airline. Then, just a few days ago, it is interfering and trying to get greater control over prices.

This is not just a series of unconnected events. It is an underlying philosophy. Now that Chifley is in office, he feels really secure, and can unleash his socialisation programme, without telling any one. He will do it by stealth, and one day we will wake up and find ourselves part of Russia.

Letters, Angry Customer. The Government wants to know how much money I have, and how I spend it. It will know this when the Bill goes through. Surely, if this Bill passes, there can be an over-riding Bill that says the Government should mind its own business, and keep its sticky hands away from little people. If I pay money to anyone, that is my business. I can even see Chifley getting up in Parliament, and saying some opposition politician has spent money on such-and-such bad thing.

The Bill was declared unconstitutional by the High Court on 11 August 1948, and this decision was upheld by the Privy Council in 1949. **Two more nails in Chifley's coffin.**

SEPTEMBER NEWS ITEMS

This is the year 1948. **The war with the Japanese ended three years ago.** But, at last, **a force of 10,000 Japanese soldiers**, hiding out in the Manchurian mountains, have **accepted the fact that Japan has lost the war, and now wish to surrender.**

As a sign that good times are ahead, it is believed that **price fixing for snakes will soon be removed**. Prior to the war, the normal unregulated price was five Shillings a foot. During the war, it rose to 15 Shillings. At that time, merchants applied to the Prices Commissioner, who then **fixed the price back at five Shillings**. It is understood that from late September, prices for snakes will no longer be regulated...

Whale prices will get similar, but different, relief. The price for whales, while it came under regulation during the war, **was not actually set at a definite level**. Now, however, to the obvious relief of all whale-sellers, **all regulations on the pricing of whales will be removed**....

Snails, again with prices undefined, **will get similar relief**.

An Australian Serviceman serving with Peace Keeping forces in Japan was, a few months ago, returned to Australia and retired from the Armed Forces because of "mental instability". **He left behind him a Japanese wife.** He attempted to join her there, but was arrested there and sent back by ship to Australia. He tried again, but was returned again....

His third attempt also failed, and he remains in custody in Japan....

This story highlights how strong was our Government's and Arthur Calwell's determination that **our racial purity should be maintained**. The policies that were set at the time made it almost impossible for **our Servicemen to have legitimate relationships, including marriage, with the Japanese**.

News reports from Tokyo suggest that some members of the agencies involved with **War Crimes are arguing that General Tojo be acquitted**. Tojo was the head of the Japanese military in the war years, and **was seen in Australia as the main arch villain**. Any suggestion that he be acquitted was an abomination to Australians, and **the news was greeted with disbelief and anger....**

However, justice was done, and **he was found guilty, and executed** on December 23rd, 1948.

King George VI will be the Royal Visitor next year, in time for the running of the Sydney Cup Race Meeting. **He will attend the Meeting**, and prize money for the Cup will be increased by 2,000 to 10,000 Pounds.

The Government issued its first fine to a Sydney butcher for **not displaying a notice in his window** offering home deliveries. **Butchers who oppose the new regulation** say that it takes a lot of money to provide home deliveries, and that more time should be provided for them to raise the capital. On the other hand, **supporters argue** that housewives have been without the service for years, and that delaying mechanisms can go on for years.

BULLYING AND DREAD

I have been trying to remember just how much bullying went on in my primary school years. I was prompted to do this by the glut of media reports that are today covering the subject. So, going back seventy years, I have been searching my memory for recollections of those supposedly carefree years. My question to myself has been "were those days in fact carefree, or where they blighted by the bullies and by fears that a small boy is prey to?"

Let me say first up that I attended a Catholic convent school, in a small coalmining town in the NSW Cessnock coalfields. There were 103 other children attending, and we were put into composite classes, so that for example, third and fourth class were stuck in together. I was a skinny little kid, who was always considered bright, so that generally I was put up into the classroom above where I should have been. This meant that I was very much underweight, and also I was not at all aggressive, so that – all other things being equal – I was a likely target for bullying. On top of that, my Mum made me wear shoes to school, and that made me conspicuous and more fun to bully.

The most obvious group of bullies who were always on hand were the so-called "retards." This far from flattering name was used for anyone who was too old for primary school, but stayed on from the age of about thirteen until he was old enough to leave school. Most of these kids were pretty thick, and were a year or more behind others of the same age. That meant for about eighteen months they formed a little clique, completely unteachable, who gave the good nuns a hard time. They always sat in the back corner, away from the rest of the class, and on a daily basis had to be told to "put it away, Mickey Malone."

Were they bullies? As far as I was concerned, not at all. Outside the classroom, they went off behind the lavatories, and bothered no one. A few dubious characters went to visit them, and generally got punched up a bit, but if you stayed on the straight and narrow path to the dunnies, you were safe. Mind you, the trip there was always a bit worrying, and the visits were always brief, just in case there was a policy change. But, for me, there was nothing of any consequence.

Then there were others, mainly boys, who were bigger and fairly mean. They were quite active when scrubbers got in their way, and pushed and shoved and abused and taunted anyone who seemed a bit odd or wet. Or, sometimes, anyone who was just there. Mind you, we had schoolyards that were virtually unsupervised, so that on many occasions the little kids ganged up on these bullies, and attacked them like willy wagtails on a crow. But in any case, these bullies were not too bad. If you stayed away from them, they were not at all mobile, and you were safe. The most you might get was a punch in the belly, a thump on the arm, or a swift trip to the earth. The only broken tooth I saw at the school, I caused myself, accidentally more or less. But for me, they gave me no problem after a few early lessons.

So, it might seem that I lived my primary school years in a fearless state. But no, that was not the case. Every day, there was the trip home from school. Going to school was no problem, because everyone just drifted in at different times. Some farm kids came in half an hour late every day,

Greenbottle-like. But going home was a different matter, with little groups wandering off together.

The first obstacle was to get past the Johnsons' house, through a spare paddock. These good people had a grown-up son, aged about twenty five, severely mentally impaired, who patrolled the fence that we had to walk past. This Billy was a frightening spectacle, with his bare feet, and the ability to jump at least twenty feet vertically into the air. And since he could not talk, he always grunted. As our group came round the corner, he would run to the fence and start grunting, grunting and grunting. In that order. He was loud too. And he would leap into the air, surely coming over the fence. But no, he would land on the upper part of it, and sit there like a bare-foot frog, never missing a grunt. To the scrubbers, he was terrifying, and they ran pell-mell past him. By the time I got to sixth class, I would walk urbanely down the block, never looking at him, and turn coolly out of his sight. I was always listening, though, for a change in the noise level. But fortunately, he remained mono-gruntic, so I never needed to flee at short notice.

Fred Ovard was a different proposition all together. Strangely, he had about the same police description as Billy Johnson, but was a lot plumper, and wore a very fashionable pair of avant garde peddle pushers, above his bare feet. But he was running loose on the street, and I do mean running. He could move faster than a randy dingo. His grunts covered about half an octave, and at times might have been interpreted as "I will squash your guts out". He would turn up at either of the two blind corners, and run straight at us, swinging his arms and grunting, normally with half a fresh wattle tree as a prop. We would scatter, often drop our school bags, and run for home. He would chase one boy until he turned and begged for mercy, and then run off after someone else.

Freddie only turned up about once a week. He obviously had a full programme terrorising the other schools in Weston and Kurri Kurri. So there was always the element of uncertainty about him turning up, and the feeling of relief when we got past Freddie's corners. I tried two devices to reduce the terror. The first one was to get ahead of the others at these corners, and then run through them. However tempted Freddie might have been to pick off this single streaker, he never did, preferring to wait for the mob. The second device did not work at all. When I was a big kid, in sixth class, and still weighing only five stone, I stood still as he launched. He came straight at me and bowled me over, then stood over me and grunted till I got up and ran away. Next day, I returned to the first device, probably moving a little faster than before.

Back at the school, however, there were three Sisters of St Joseph who did a lot to keep the level of fear at a suitably high level. In my first few years, there was a Sister Pius. She always carried, or so I remember, a 15-inch ruler, and rapped knuckles with it. My fear of her was only on Friday afternoons, in our so-called fun sessions. During the rest of the week, I was safe from rapping, because I was a bright student, and well behaved. The good Sister was quite reasonable, and so left me alone then.

Friday afternoons were different. Here we pursued intellectually stimulating activities such as cutting out rosellas and baskets of fruit from the labels on jam tins, and pasting them onto cardboard. Or we made pretty weaving patterns from coloured paper. My trouble was that I was at least a year younger than the others in the class, and my motor skills were a mile behind theirs. So I messed up all the time. The good Sister's problem was that she did not understand this, and she got very frustrated when her star pupil failed in these simple pursuits. So she nagged me "Ronnie Williams, I know you can do it; why are you being so stubborn?" And then would come a rap or two. I suppose they were just gentle raps, mere tokens. But they impressed me as something to avoid; and since I could do nothing about them, I just settled out to hate Friday afternoons.

Sister Ann was different. She was, or appeared to me, just plain mean. Again, I was often immune from her violence because of my mental abilities and my conduct. Now, however, we were learning to write, with pen and ink. We were using pens with nibs, and ink that came in ink-wells. Spillages and blots were everywhere. Nibs were always clogging up with hair and paper fibre. They were always breaking. Cecil Smith once got his big toe caught in the neck of the big bottle that fed the ink-wells, and contrived to have it there all day. Writing lessons were always chaotic.

Again, my physical capabilities lagged behind the rest of the older class. So again, I frustrated the good Sister, and so she belted me. I suppose I am exaggerating, but that nun had an 18-inch ruler that was heavy, and we sinners had to take the cuts on our bare hands. The thing that got to me was the sheer malevolence that she showed while caning. I was always the Teacher's Pet, and, apart from writing, could do no wrong. But when it came to physical violence, she looked like she meant it, and that she really got sadistic pleasure from it.

I do not know whether these two encounters constitute bullying, in today's sense. It doesn't matter really. But the fear that they engendered was always with me up till this point in Primary school. To use medical terms, this was not acute fear; rather, a low-grade chronic fear. One that, though always there with me in the classroom, did not make me sweat until the nun started to walk up my aisle. Looking back, I know that this was not at all good for me; but I suspect that every child has his own Sister Monica in one form or another. Perhaps it is part and parcel of childhood. Perhaps parents, who try to save their children from all such experiences, just create other Anns, then or saved up till later. How would I know?

The greatest source of dread for me was the fear of God, and what he might do to me. The good nuns, and the visiting priests, were always talking about God's wrath. Every week, at least, we would get graphic pictures of how we would suffer if we sinned even a little. If we sinned a lot, if we committed a mortal sin, we would be sent to Hell. This, for those who sadly missed out on the indoctrination, was a place of eternal torment, with fire and brimstone as the most common backdrop, and a hearty, unquenched thirst. If you enjoyed this type of thing, that was fine, because it went on forever. But if you did not, and I thought it would not be all that good, the idea of it filled me with constant dread.

So, I was always vigilant about avoiding mortal sins. I can tell you that through my primary school years, I did not commit any rapes, murders, robberies, adultery, or the many other sins that were mortal. Further I avoided other sins, which even though not so conspicuous, were sins against the Church, and also mortal. Every time I went to Mass, three times a week, I cleaned my teeth before going. Did I let a single drop of water go down my gullet? Certainly not. Did I have even a crumb from the sponge cake with cream on the kitchen table? The very suggestion is insulting. What about meat on Friday, and fasting in Lent? Let me just say that I always did the right thing.

So, mortal-sinless, I should have rested well at night. But that was not the case. The pictures painted were so bad, and painted so often that they were constantly with me, always loitering with the Devil in the background. There was always the fear that I would suffer the fate of innumerable people, who live a blameless life, until one day they sinned. Then God, in his wisdom, struck them down with lightning, or fire, or a sudden disease that sometimes made their hands fall off. And there they were, with no prior convictions, registering for Hell.

All of this dread piled up when the Redemptrist Fathers came to town. Every two years, this travelling troupe would visit our town for a "Mission". They would spend their days visiting lapsed Catholics, and stay with that lucky person, until he committed to go to the Mission service one day soon. Then, in the evenings, those services were held. There was only an hour allocated for these, so no time was wasted on this love-of-God stuff or love-thy-neighbour rubbish. It was all Hell, brimstone, groaning and gnashing of teeth, all-consuming thirsts, and glasses of ginger beer just out of reach. The aim was to terrify everyone, to make them mend their sinful ways, and come back to the fold. My three adult cousins, Tich, Frankie and Digger were always suitably terrified, and afterwards would come and get Dad so they could go to the pub and laugh it off.

I was an altar boy, so I served at all fourteen of these friendly get-togethers. By the time the Mission was finished, I could tell you the entire script, though I would have had trouble telling the wrenching story of the poor little boy whose hand trembled so close to that icy cold ginger beer.

I wonder now whether this systematic heightening of dread in people has had any lasting effect on them. If I googled "Catholic, Hell, phobia, psychiatry, bullying", or something like it, would I get a flood of positives that tell of permanent damage? Would I find that there are psychopaths out there who now give their victims Chinese water torture, using ginger beer instead of water? I also wonder about whether the indoctrination I got had any results that were beneficial to me. As I look at it now, I cannot see any. I did get training in all the values that are important to all of us, and in the way to live a modest life in our liberal society. But, in terms of bullying and dread, I can see no purpose for them, and I would have been happier and better off without them.

YOUR LOYAL SUBJECTS

Arthur Calwell was currently the Minister for Shipping in the Labor government. He was one of the strongest proponents of the White Australia Policy, and was very Left Wing on other issues. At about this time, he was having trouble with Britain over shipping and other matters, and he wandered round muttering about the dangers of the Empire disintegrating, and what a loss it would be if Australia left the British Empire. But this was sheer rubbish. His was a lonely voice, and this nation was still staunchly British, almost to the core.

Of course, this loyalty was to the British nation itself, and to its people. And it was loyalty to the Crown, and the Royal family, and all that went with it. All of the doings of the King and Queen, and Elizabeth and Margaret, were reported and photographed in full, not just by the women's magazines, but also by the daily newspapers. Royal occasions were fully reported. Such grand events as engagements, marriages, overseas tours, births, and deaths were given front page status, and stayed on that page until the last drop of public interest had been milked. Even a windy day at the races was news. Lords and Ladies and Knights were always good for filling a vacant spot on a page, and any talk of a romance was welcomed with glee. Princess Margaret's dalliances were later reported in full but, in those days, in respected and awed tones. In short, this side of our loyalty to Britain was fully secure, and the proponents of a republic were not heard, if they existed at all.

In 1948, Elizabeth had been married to Phillip late the previous year. The King and Queen were due to tour Australia in 1949. Elizabeth, pregnant by now, was destined to give birth to Charles in late 1948. And sadly, the King would die in a few years and, of course, Elizabeth would succeed him.

The intense interest in the Royals was not restricted to the members of the Household. Anybody with a title was fair game. The Duchess of Gloucester, who had been living in

Australia as the wife of the Governor General but had now gone back to England, still had 22 photos appear in the major morning newspapers in 1948. Viscount Montgomery, now retiring as the Viceroy of India, had even more. Lady Baden Powell, when she visited here, captured the headlines everywhere she went, and reminded us that the scouting movement was more ubiquitous then that it is now.

Lady Beveridge, the wife of a leading economist, was given celebrity status on her sojourn in Sydney. Without being disrespectful, it is true to say that the Press **now** would not give a hoot what an English Lady thought of Australia. But, at the time, it made us feel good when she said nice things.

Lady Beveridge, relaxed after a days' shopping, told a Press conference today that she loved the brilliance and colour of Sydney's shops. "I bought a few colourful accessories and one beautiful cream three-quarter length lambs-wool coat. I intend to buy some New Look fashions in Melbourne. If I have any money left", she chuckled.

"Australian girls look so fresh and colourful, and are very different from our own girls, who have to wear drab austerity models. The food here has been a glimpse of the past. To-day we had a Vienna schnitzel, which had more veal in it than we get in a week's ration in London.

"Sydney, though, is very noisy. It is a sad thing in a young city that the roar of trams should deafen me from dawn to midnight in a suite nine floors above the street. All young cities are the same. They won't learn from the mistakes of London and New York. You cannot build a stable society unless you conquer noise".

Ten years later, after the Menzies fiasco in Egypt, and then later still with Macmillan's "winds of change" policies, and after we opened our borders to non-British migrants, Australia started to drift away from regarding Britain as the Mother Country. But, right now in 1948, for us, it was still the Land of Hope and Glory.

CHIPS RAFFERTY

This gentleman was first famous for his acting role in the film *Forty Thousand Horsemen*. It came to my home at the Centre of the Universe, Abermain, at the end of the War, and was heralded by a great deal of publicity.

I think I was the typical boy of the times. I had been brought up during the War, had read of the bombings, had helped build an air-raid shelter in my backyard, and a slit trench in the clay of the school yard. I had watched fifty war movies, seen all the Americans each week win the War single-handed, and rejoiced when Audie Murphy handed out major damage to the Japanese in Bataan.

So it was not surprising that when I heard that *Forty Thousand Horsemen* was coming to Abermain, and what's more, that Chips Rafferty would be there in person, it was a matter for great excitement. All my dreams about throwing grenades into enemy dugouts, about smoking out caveloads full of Japanese with a flame thrower, and destroying a convoy of Panzer tanks with a bazooka, seemed to have substance. Here was a chance to see a great War hero, the man who really represented the active face of War in this country.

So when Chips turned up at the Star Theatre I was agog. He came in straight away, and without looking directly at the audience, gave a three minute speech on supporting War bonds, and now Peace bonds, and left. No dead bodies, no accounts of slaughters, no stories of escapes from plumes of deadly gas. Just those bloody Bonds.

What a disappointment. How could this great man talk such rubbish? How could he show so little interest in us all, and especially me? You might get the idea that he was just an ordinary man, just an actor, say. And what about his movie? Well, it turned out to be a big wet blanket as well. Lots of actors in military uniform talking, and hardly any of those splendid scenes of pitched hand-to-hand fighting that I had expected. A bad movie, and a bad day.

When I got home, everything came good again. My head re-entered the clouds. It turned out that Chips was doing a circuit of four theatres that afternoon, and we were the last one he visited. But he had to do them in the reverse order in the evening. So he had to wait in Abermain till seven-thirty.

Where did he wait? At the Denman Hotel, Abermain. Where did my Dad drink on Saturday afternoons? At the Denman Hotel, Abermain. So home he came at seven-fifteen, happy as Larry, because he had spent the afternoon drinking with Chips Rafferty. I too could not have been happier. My Dad drinking all afternoon with the greatest fighter this county could ever produce, with the man who led forty thousand horses to a glorious victory in the deserts of Arabia, with the hero to end all heroes. What a Dad. What a real hero. My social life was now secure forever. What a Dad.

As for Chips, it turned out that he **was** in fact an actor. He went on over the next few years to star in *The Overlanders* and *The Eureka Stockade*.

OCTOBER NEWS ITEMS

Police at **Goondiwindi** in outback NSW believe a firebug has **set eight fires at woolsheds in the last month**. Kerosene has been used at some sites, and water supply has been choked at many sites. All blazes have started after midnight, and threatening letters have been received by graziers....

Last night the railway station at the railhead Talwood was burned to the ground. **Graziers believe that the villain responsible aims to disrupt the wool industry....**

Comment. These were years when **the prosperity of the nation rested on the sheep's back. Any threat to the industry's viability was big news.**

Three telephone linesmen were electrocuted and killed in Melbourne when a line they were handling was crossed by a high-voltage cable that had come free.

The Press is full every day with **reported threats of a Third World War**, and how Russia - the villain - was plotting to destroy the goodies, the US and Britain. Half the front pages of newspapers were focused on this prospect. To keep the excitement going, **the US Director of Civil Defense has issued a plan covering mass evacuation and relief of war stricken cities....**

It also covers press and radio censorship, prices and wages control, rationing of food and scarce commodities, and man-power mobilisation. Remember **the US was spared all of these in WWII, while Australia and Britain suffered severely from them....**

As you well know, **such plans were not necessary**. But, as you might also appreciate, **similar scare stories still (70 years later) dominate our front pages** and, fortunately, most of them never happen either.

In Paris, **the wife of a leading Communist Trade Union official**, accompanied by 250 women, marched to the home of **the manager of the local steelworks** and forced him to the town square where 6,000 workers were waiting. He was then marched three miles, and imprisoned for three hours in the cokery. Local police did not intervene....

This is an example of **the growth of Communism that was spreading across France and Italy**. It promised that the Reds, apart from fixing the world, **would also intervene in local affairs and find fixes for them.**

The Reds were not far from controversy in Australia, either. In Melbourne, it was their custom to meet on Sunday afternoons on the Yarra Bank for a morale booster. **This weekend, a small mob of ex-Servicemen, opposed to the Reds, disrupted their meeting** by using loudspeakers to play "God Save the King", and shouting slogans such as "Are you Communists or British?" **A few punch-ups started**, and the van of the ex-Servicemen was almost overturned....

More punch-ups amid much shouting of "Fascist pigs" and "Heil Hitler", the van escaped killing no one, and the Servicemen vowed that they would be back next week. **No real harm was done, but such events occurred all over Australia regularly in one form or another.**

LOVE ME SAILOR

The Criminal Court today found Robert Shaw Close, and his publisher Georgian Books, guilty of having written and published an obscene book, entitled *Love Me Sailor*. While it was a jury verdict, Mr Justice Martin said he agreed with it. **He refused bail**, pending sentence. He explained that "a man who was responsible for this work cannot quibble if he is sent to gaol."

A para on this book. About a nymphomaniac on board a windjammer on a longish voyage. The sexual developments in the book were presented by insinuation alone, and left all the gory bits to the imagination of the reader. The main objection to the book was its language. Lewd language and blasphemy were used off and on to describe situations that arose, but in fact the book got nowhere near the language that would have been used in such actual situations. It was a question of whether a writer could use real language, or had to use artificially nice language. Nowadays, some books seem to contain nothing but "real" language, but back in 1948, this was a serious contest between very different schools of thought.

Two years earlier, in Sydney, the writer Lawson Glassop, was prosecuted for writing a novel called *We Were the Rats*. In this case, he was tried by a magistrate without the aid of a jury, and the evidence against him was provided by a police sergeant who was completely ignorant of literature. In my 1946 book, I reviewed it thus: "Looking back seventy years, and considering the sorts of material now available to readers, and to viewers of films and television, the book seems in no way offensive. There were two thrusts to the prosecution's arguments. Firstly, the use of the word "bloody," and some minor blasphemy. Secondly, on two pages, there was a discussion of sexual encounters in a frank manner, that would nowadays not raise an eyebrow in the *Women's Weekly*. But they did then, and hence the prosecutions."

The book told an entertaining story about soldiers in WWII who at one stage were sent to Trobruk. Glassop's argument was that he had to make the book realistic, and to do that, had to correctly portray the conversations of his characters. If he sanitised the book, if he expressed thoughts using **artificial language that no soldier in reality would use**, then he would be ignoring the harsh reality that he was describing. Glassop was fined a little, and so too were his publishers. The book got great publicity, so that in one sense, Glassop gained from the heavy-handed intervention.

This "Love Me" trial was quite different. It was conducted before a jury, and it must be assumed that they reflected the views of the wider community. Another point of difference is that this time when he was found guilty, **he was not bailed, but held in prison**.

There were many people who were outraged at all this. Some of these argued for realism in literature, and said that Close's portrayal was a welcome relief from the make-believe that bookstores were filled with. Some were critical of the process whereby an author was not to portray a scene as he saw it, but as some goody-goody fantasy. Further, it was argued that Close had toned down his descriptions, and the reality would have been much more provocative. More still were shocked by his imprisonment. The indignation was strongest in Melbourne, but many angry Letters found their way into the Sydney pages.

Letters, Muir Holburn. As President of the Fellowship of Australian Writers, I wish to add my voice to the mounting expressions of indignation at the prosecution of Robert Close by the Victorian government. Those, in particular, who care for the fair reputation of Australia overseas, will surely be dismayed at the feelings of contempt and ridicule that these uncivilised proceedings are likely to invoke in countries where there pertains a more practical regard for freedom of expression.

It should be noted that the law under which Robert Close has been prosecuted is both antiquated and unique, being among a minority of advanced countries wherein such intolerable obstacles are placed in the path of creative artists.

As though the legal action against this author were not a sufficient outrage, we have also had to witness the spectacle of Robert Close, a man of fine mind but delicate condition, being subjected to the humiliating treatment usually accorded to violent criminals. Mr Whatmore, Victorian Inspector of Prisons, in one of his reported statements, all of which possess a partisan flavour remarkable in the utterances of a Public Servant, has stated that any differentiation in the treatment of prisoners is not permissible, regardless of the prisoner's offence.

These questions will not, I suggest, remain matters of indifference to those Australians who retain an innate sense of balance and decency.

Letters, A Hannan. Your correspondent, Mr Muir Holburn, claims that Mr Close should never have been prosecuted, and that the laws to do so were antiquated and unique.

May I point out that the law referred to is a law against the publication of obscene and indecent matter, and is intended for the protection of the community, especially young people. As Crown Solicitor of South Australia, I had to institute prosecutions in that State against booksellers who sold Mr Close's book.

Does your correspondent want the law repealed or does he want authors and writers exempted from its operation? If so, the purpose of the law will be partially frustrated, and there will be a privileged class in the community, consisting of authors and novelists, who will be allowed by law to publish obscene and indecent matter in their books, while the humble scribbler on walls in public places will be liable to penalties under the law.

Regarding the claim by your correspondent that the law is unique, the answer is that the law under discussion is in force in every Australian State, in England, in New Zealand, in the US, and every country in which Christian principles are still honoured.

Letters, Herbert Harrison. One is delighted to read that a very serious view has been taken of obscene publications. The downward trend of writers and publishers has been noticeable for a long time. Some recent publications contain references from which any decent parent would shelter a growing son or daughter.

Give us wholesome, educational, and moral-building writings, and commit the filthy matter to where it rightly belongs – the gutter.

Letters, John O'Rockie. As a life member of Australian Writers, I query the right of Muir Holburn to speak on behalf of the Fellowship. As far as my personal experience goes, the members of that group have not been canvassed for their opinions.

I assume that the idea behind most of the fuss now being made about what is really mental garbage is in defence of what has euphemistically been described as a liberal expression of opinion. Too much is heard and read of rights, and too little about the duties and responsibilities to the community. I, for one, protest against the indiscriminate exercise of licence under the guise of liberty. Liberty means discipline, it means the duty to maintain standards and deliberately avoid giving offence to others who might have different standards but still deserve a place on this earth.

Letters, James Martin. This week, Australia is celebrating 100 years of progress in culture and education, having reached a stage of medieval barbarity which permits the burning of dogs alive at a cost of 250 pound a time, and the handcuffing and imprisonment of authors. We have reached an age where policemen and Customs officials tell us what we may, and may not, read. We offer such encouragement to culture that our talent in literature, music and art, flee the country at the earliest opportunity.

Australia is rapidly becoming the laughing stock of the world, and I suggest that my fellow authors should rise up in arms and replace public apathy with a firm resolve to rid themselves of bumbledom, archaic laws, and power-drunk buccaneers, who are daily finding fresh regressions and methods of grinding us aground.

Letters, Peter Cline. Mr A Hannan, in his letter, overlooks the fact that the law on the matter is in a state of obvious and dynamic change. For example, in NSW, there is a new legislative amendment under review as a "works of art" amendment for liberalising the law. Also judicially, in NSW, the amendment proposes that a conviction will bring only a fine, and not imprisonment. A law that is thus doddering on the shaky ground of an altering public and legislative opinion should not, in justice, be as ruthlessly enforced as the law of larceny or fraud.

Mr Hannan also overlooks the fact that authors are actually a privileged class. To regard our young literary talent as potential scribblers on walls, to suspect and scrutinise every word they write, to treat them as criminals if a word or two can be torn from their context and displayed as "obscene," is to take the attitude as narrow and parochial as it is dangerous to cultural horizons.

Letters, G McMahon. I believe that the public must be protected against literature that has pornography as its theme. The best evidence that Mr Close's book fell into that category was the Court evidence that the book was selling for five pounds on the black market. Without doubt, those who were willing to pay that sum were not lovers of good literature.

The handcuffing was unfortunate, even unnecessary, but I don't think Mr Close will suffer physically as a result. Let us hope that his sensitive mind (Mr Holburn's description) will focus towards literature that will be fit and educational for healthy and intelligent-minded people.

Close was ultimately released from Pentridge Gaol on bail, because his lawyer had argued that his case was heard before the wrong court. His hearing had been before the Practice Court, which released him, on 50 Pounds bail, pending the hearing of his appeal against his sentence. A few months later, his appeal was unsuccessful, but he was not jailed again.

LAURENCE OLIVIER

In Winter, Sir Laurence Olivier and his wife Vivienne Leigh toured Australia and New Zealand, and they stayed here for five months. Olivier was married to this lady in 1940, and had been knighted in 1947. He had recently starred in the British production of *Hamlet*, and on the back of that great success, played to Australia in *Richard III* and *School for Scandal*. Leigh had earlier won an Oscar for her role in *Gone with the Wind*. The couple divorced in 1960, and he was granted a peerage in 1970. He died in 1989.

To say that this divine couple took Australia by storm would be a complete understatement. They had rave reviews every time they performed, and were mobbed every time they appeared for a public outing. Remember that it all went on for months.

Sadly, however, for this brilliant couple, there was trouble afoot, and their marriage was close to the rocks. They did divorce a dozen years later, after several years of unhappiness together, and somewhat **marred the fairy-tale image that they had spent years generating**.

JOHN HENRY AUSTRAL

This illustrious gentleman was a **fictional** character created by the Liberal Party. He was placed in a normal home situation with a regular cast of characters, and these persons reacted with John once or twice week to create an ongoing radio serial. It was similar in set-up to *Martin's Corner*, or the even more famous *Dad and Dave*. The whole series was cleverly conceived, because it picked up on the dominant form of Australian cultural life, the radio serial, at a time when it was widely accepted here.

The main difference was that, given its creator, it was intended to push the barrow of the Liberal Party by satirising the people and policies of the Labor Party, and at the same time extolling the virtues of the Liberals. Much of the conversations were benign, but when it went into satire, it was quite funny and very cutting, and apparently most effective. At least, among the Liberals. The episodes railed against Labor's plan to socialise the world, and against waiting in queues, and later on, the menace of Communism. The critical parts were almost as biting as the five minute slots on Thursday night on the ABC (from 2007), when the late John Clarke and Brian Dawe cut loose.

The Labor Party, as the Government, wanted to somehow stop this flow of damaging propaganda. At the end of 1948 it was preparing to make some necessary changes to the Broadcasting Act (1942) because of technological and social changes that were happening then. So it decided to strengthen part of the new Act, **to place restraints on political satire on air**. Of course, it was the *Austral* satires that it had in its sights.

Not everyone appreciated this breach of free speech, and in the Letters pages, many of them said so. I enclose a sample.

Letters, Edith Shortland. If the Federal Government has the right to dictate to broadcasting services the nature of their programmes, it can proscribe criticism of politicians, and prescribe to newpaper editors the publicity they should give to political leaders.

One bank, one broadcast system, one newspaper, to be followed by one political party with perpetual power, and we have followed the example of Russia and its subservient States. Perhaps many of the actions of the

Labor Party can be explained by the fact that it wants to become the **perpetual** government in Australia.

Is there to be no restriction on the Government's determination to encroach further on our liberties? We have had sufficient warnings. The time for action is now. For centuries, freedom of speech and thought has been recognised as the inalienable right of every Britisher, provided he does not offend the law of libel.

Letters, Iris Hyde. The Bill to make changes in the control of broadcasting follows a technique only too familiar in many enslaved countries of Europe. That is, the technique of suppression.

The plain fact is that this legislation is mainly aimed at control of anti-socialist broadcasts like John Henry Austral, and Country Quiz, which find favour with a large section of the listening public.

Commercial stations have already a vital interest in ensuring suitable programmes with appeal to listeners, because without that appeal they would lose first their listeners, and second their sponsors.

Unless citizens realise the present trend and act accordingly, a time is fast approaching when we shall read only those books and newspapers, and see only those plays, and hear only those broadcasts, which a totalitarian government permits us to read, see, and hear.

Letters, Kathleen Gavin. It is easily seen that the Government is determined to carry out its nationalisation plans. The proposed Broadcasting Bill is the latest insult to the public's intelligence.

Senator Cameron says that he means to see that the public gets more than Jazz and race results "from one end of the dial to the other." He was not very concerned when the Loan broadcasts were forced upon the listening public "from one end of the dial to the other."

Perhaps he considered that those programmes were such masterpieces of universal appeal that nobody would dream of listening to any other. Or was it just a preview of what we would expect if this radio dictatorship comes into being.

Letters, RECENTLY RETIRED. The parts of the new Broadcasting Act that place restrictions on free speech are to be deplored. For years I worked as a public servant, and at times I occupied quite senior positions, and I have seen ministers do anything they can to stifle any sort of criticism.

Quite recently I saw a senior Minister, who is a very heavy smoker, sitting at a table with some other people. One of these, a junior in rank, said he would not work over some charts with the Minister. When pressed to say why not, he said it was because the Minister's clothes stank of tobacco and smoke. The Minister was furious, and the junior was ejected. But it was clear to everyone that this Minister stank to High Heavens, and it was he who should have been dispatched.

I tell you this because it shows that there are many politicians who cannot take criticism, even when it is obviously true. They think, when they hear John Henry Austral, that these remarks are going to a million people, and whether they are true or not, people who do not know better will form their impressions from them. If they happen to be true, then it makes it harder to convince anyone that you have a case to put, especially if you do not have a radio programme of your own.

I want to add that I have seen Ministers from both sides of Government come and go. But they are all the same. They want to be painted as Saints, and have no criticism that they hear. It does not matter what Party they are from. If the Labor Party was doing this to the Liberals, then it would be the Liberals bringing down the legislation. Pots calling kettles black comes to mind.

Letters, Mary Tukoni. We love listening to the John Henry Austral wireless show. It makes us all laugh a lot. We laugh because what they say is clever and funny at times. But we also laugh because the white men who want us to listen want our votes. But we do not have any votes because we are aborigines. And aborigines do not get votes because they are black, and so we don't get anything. Do the men who put on this show ever think about how many more votes they could get if we got to vote, and voted for them?

Letters, C Hemmingway. It was not in support of this sort of legislation that the people voted at the last election. The intention of the Labor leaders to stifle free speech and free trade were carefully concealed during the election campaign.

If this Government has its way, it will not be long before we will see newspaper columnists, cartoonists, and stage and radio comedians who crack political jokes, being hauled off to concentration camps. When he goes off to the polls next year, let no Australian worthy of the name forget this latest attempt to enslave him.

Result. The Labor Party had a hard time with this in Parliament. There was much to attack. For example, Section 22 was proposing that **all political commentary would be forbidden** on air for a period covering the last five years. Mr E Harrison, Acting Leader of the Opposition, argued that it was five years ago that the Government first made its socialisation plans public, and this brought further ridicule on the proposed Act. Eventually, the Minister for Information, Mr Calwell, stated that the Act would not prohibit a person on air making an attack on a parliamentarian, provided that the person who makes the statement can be identified, and takes responsibility for it. With this, the modified Act was passed, in a much watered-down fashion. To my knowledge, no prosecutions were launched under it.

Comment. In 2018, you will still notice that at the end of political ads, there is always an addendum that says "authorised by so so, of such and such a group."

NEWS AND VIEWS

Do you remember these widely advertised products.?

Sydney Flour. Did you use it every day. For scones and cakes that mother makes. And did you find that it's OK?

Peters Ice Cream. It appears that you were always within reach of this delicious and refreshing ice cream. Keep in mind, if in doubt, that Peters is an important energy food, it repairs physical wear and tear, at the same time as it builds extra muscles and stamina.

Arnott's Famous Biscuits. Scotch Fingers, Iced Vo-Vos and Monte Carlos. Remember, there is no Substitute of Quality.

If you have a cut in an accident, there is always available **an Iodine bottle in your Medicine Chest.** This potion is good for rheumatism, influenza, sore throat, chilblains, sore feet, wounds, sprains, cuts, scratches, and splinters.

And you can get all the energy you need through **I**nner **Cleanliness** by swallowing a dose of **Andrews Liver Salts**. This is especially for housewives doing their onerous chores.

NOVEMBER NEWS ITEMS

November 1st. Two great races were at the post, ready to go on the same day.

The *New York Times* predicted that **Thomas Dewey**, now Governor of New York State, **would be elected President of the USA**. It thought that the College of Electors would vote **345 to 105 in favour of Dewey**....

Meanwhile back in Melbourne, the odds are that the New Zealand horse, *Howe*, will win **the Melbourne Cup**. Punters are so confident that the giant will be first past the post that the horse is now **at short odds-on**. This favourite is so popular that **betting on the race has virtually ceased.**

November 2nd. A reminder that there were serious matters affecting the world came from **China**, with news that, since February 2, the Nationalist Generalismo Chiang Kai Shek had his armies poised inside the Great Wall **ready for a deciding battles against Mao's Communists.** This war had raged for more than a decade, **with American-backed Chiang now just hanging on. The end for him might well be nigh.**

A legless Digger living in Brisbane thought he would enjoy the **warmer climate in Cairns**, so he got in his wheel chair and **pushed himself 1,500 miles to that fair township. He accepted no help, and refused all lifts that were offered.** He had trouble moving on a few mountains, so he then got out and, on his knees, pushed the wheel chair ahead of him. **He arrived in good health. The trip took 88 days.**

November 4th. A crowd of 101,000 saw outsider *Rimfire* win the Cup. The jockey was 15-year-old Ray Neville....

All the experts were wrong, and all the punters were wrong. The winner was such an outsider that the *SMH* reporter stated that people round the course were looking at each other and asking "Who was **that**?" **Not a good day for the punters.**

It was no better for punters in America. The venerable *New York Times* **newspaper was wrong and** the **incumbent, Harry Truman, had a comfortable win** of 304 to 299 Electoral votes. The Democrats also won the battle for the House, so they are in the happy position of having **at least two years control of the Legislature**.

In   China, Chiang Kai Shek's Nationalist armies suffered severe defeats in the last few days. Shanghai is now close to the battle front, and starvation for that city's five million people is imminent. Even with US help, there seems no hope for Chiang....

Comment. Early next year, **he and his forces left the mainland and settled in Taiwan**, where he persisted in his futile attempts to make a comeback. Throughout this period, **America backed him, and the enmity generated at that time still pervades Chinese-American relations today.**

About this time, **sloppy joes** came to Australia. They were sometimes called wind cheaters. Do you remember what they were? Do you remember what a "**sheila**" was? .... Well, what about a **zac**?

PALESTINE AND INDIA

Both of these countries were hotspots. Britain was exhausted, both emotionally and financially, from WWII, and wanted to get out of overseas commitments, move its troops and its administration back home, and leave these two countries in particular to their own devices. It had established withdrawal plans, and in 1948, the plans were being implemented with much haste.

In Palestine, the native population was being flooded with Jews from all over the world, but particularly by devastated European Jews, seeking a new homeland. The situation had deteriorated to the stage where the Arabs and the Jews were conducting terrorist attacks against each other, and the few remaining British were being caught in the middle. The other Arab states were getting more involved, in half-hearted actions against the Jews, but their efforts were close to useless because they were not at all co-ordinated, and indeed they all had their own incompatible aims. **Big troubles were brewing.**

For example, in early November, a huge explosion occurred in Jerusalem at day-break in the most fashionable shopping centre in the middle of the city. *Haganah* reports indicate that about 75 people were killed. Among the dead were three British military personnel.

The explosives were carried in three lorries up the main street and were then detonated. It was claimed that men in uniform were seen running from the vehicle, and the suggestion was that they were British. Hysterical Jews then began scouring the streets with rifles, pistols and grenades, looking for the culprits, now assumed to be British.

The Jewish terrorist organisation, Irgun Ini Leumi, later issued a statement that "henceforth all British troops or police entering Jewish sections of Jerusalem would be executed." Crowds made threats to the rescue workers who helped with the carnage, and made their work dangerous and difficult.

Then again, forces from a combination of Arab nations last night shelled Jerusalem. More than 40 shells landed on the city, and four Jews were killed. This was the first time the city has been shelled in Jerusalem's history.

Comment. These were not just isolated incidents. Almost every day, such tragedies occurred. The question was still whether hostilities would generate into a full-scale war (they did), or whether matters could be settled by negotiation. In fact, the chance of that happening was small, since both the Arabs and the Jews wanted to get rid of the others completely from their one bit of land. Anyway, for the rest of the year, cease-fire talks were often held, and these were interspersed with periods of active and violent hostilities, against a background of mutual terrorism. Gradually, as atrocities on both sides were committed **and remembered**, all hopes of peace went out the window, and full scale war came in 1949.

DEATH OF GANDHI

In India, the British had departed in about August, 1947, and India had been partitioned. Strangely, it was divided into three geographic parts. The central part remained India, and its population was to be mainly Hindu. The two wings, in the north-east and the north-west, became East and West Pakistan respectively, though these two separated parts were to function as one nation. This new nation was destined to adhere to the Muslim religion. There was no compulsion to move from one nation to the other, but to remain, say, a Muslim in a population of Hindus was rife with danger. At least seventeen million moved in the first two years. For the next year and more, well into 1948, the nations were in turmoil as these vast numbers moved to their new homeland.

The dislocation for all parties was extreme, and violence often ensued. **Some** of this was purely local, as factions within towns clashed, and **some** of it was at the level of organised armies. **Over one million people died** as result of violence in this period, with both religions suffering terrible losses. The two main religions suffered equally. The murder of Mahatma Gandhi on **January 30**, 1948, had only exacerbated the problem.

News Report, January 31, New Delhi. The Mahatma Gandhi, aged 78, was assassinated on his way to his regular prayer meeting in New Delhi today. He was shot three times, once in the body and twice in the torso. He was carried swiftly to the house of an industrialist friend, where he died without speaking. The assassin, a Hindu Communist, was arrested by police. He tried to commit suicide, but the bullet only grazed his forehead.

The above report carried the news that the killer was a Communist. This was the order of the day, to accuse bad guys everywhere of being a Red. As it turned out, he was a devout Hindu, aged 35, disturbed by the conflict with the Muslims, and he blamed Ghandi for that. In Court, he read out a five-hour statement, in which he pointed out that before he fired the shots, he bowed in reverence to Ghandi. He claimed that the holy man's policies had resulted in the emasculation of the Hindu community, and the vivisection of India. He claimed that Gandhi's actions had brought ruin to millions of Hindus. "The only effective way to relieve the Hindus from Moslem atrocities was to remove Ghandi from this world."

LATER THAT YEAR IN INDIA

The death of Gandhi left India without the astute leadership that tempered angry spirits in the nation. So, as the year progressed, enmity between the religious groups grew and grew, and by the end of the year, the nation was sadly in a state of bitter upheaval.

But problems were not restricted to conflicts between the two major religions. The nation was made up of States, and in this period of extreme disruption, conflicts within India between States were common. For example, Hyderabad, in the middle of India, wanted to remain Muslim, and was convinced of the folly of this only by the military interventions of its neighbours that cost thousands of lives.

News item, Calcutta, November. Savage Hindu-Moslem rioting, said to be the worst in India's history, has plunged eastern Bengal into turmoil. Armed and fanatical mobs, 20,000 strong, are reported to be carrying fire and sword through an area of 250 square miles in the Noakhali district. Twenty five thousand people are fleeing from the fury of the mobs, and 10,000 have taken refuge in Chandipur, which Ghurka troops are preparing to defend if necessary.

Comment. Day after day such reports came out of India for two years before any signs of true peace were observable. Pakistan was in an even worse state, and has continued to this day to be unstable. **Firstly**, it was plagued by being divided into two parts, East and West, with a thousand miles of Indian territory between them.

Second, in the first few years, when it needed strong leadership, its leading political figures died. Jinnah, who had been appointed Governor General, died in 1948. Patel, the political founder of Parkistan, died in 1950. Liaqat Ali Khan, the first Prime Minister, was assassinated three years later. The whole first few years were marked by political squabbling about a constitution, and by corruption, and by endless disputes as candidates jockeyed for key positions. By 1958, the situation had become hopeless and the military intervened, and that marks the beginning of the military rule that determined the fate of the nation for much of the subsequent years.

CRICKET AND SPORT

After the War, cricket took up at about where it had left off in 1940. All of the administration that supported the game was still in place, so it was a case of electing new officials and getting on with the job of resurrecting cricket round the nation.

An important part of this was international cricket. In 1946, the so-called Services team had toured Australia. This was a group of talented Australian cricketers who had served in the military forces, mainly in England and Europe, and who had at times been released to form part of an Australian team that played against Services teams from other countries. Several members had in fact been part of the Australian Test team pre-war, and the others were just about as good as these. After the War, this team toured our nation, and stopped in each capital city except Perth, and played a 4-day match against the newly-picked State teams. For me, aged 12 at the time, this was my introduction to First-Class cricket, and it suffices to say that the willow entered my soul at that time, and has never left it.

The following year the English team came out, and we managed to wallop them, and in the long school holidays of 1947, we also walloped the Indians.

But now in 1948, it was said in some quarters, we were off to England to play against a national team that had had time to recover from its severe war-time losses. The Australian team was the so-called Invincibles, and many still claim it was the greatest team ever. No one will ever convince me, a 14-year-old fanatic at the time, that any other team will ever come within cooee of it.

These Invincibles romped through the County sides, and added all sorts of records to the books. Batsmen like Bradman, Miller, Barnes, and Brown had a run-fest. Then bowlers like Lindwall and Miller, and Bill Johnston did it all with ball.

Then it came to the Test Matches. **Here I must digress from the team back into my bedroom in Abermain.** The ABC radio began broadcasting the Tests, starting about 10.30 in the evenings, for half an hour, and then, after Lunch, they often broadcast through the night till four in the morning. Being a young lad, and not yet much addicted to booze and wild women, I was generally all tucked in by nine o'clock. So, it seemed unlikely that I would get parental blessing to listen all the way through till stumps each day. So, to coin a phrase from today, I "brokered a deal."

My parents said I could listen up to Lunch on the family radio. And then that great big box had to go off. But they knew that I would die a horrible death every day unless I heard every ball bowled. So rather than having to bury me every morning, they said I could listen on my crystal set. This neat little device, which in the spirit of the times I built myself, could pick up 2NC, and give me a ball-by-ball description of the entire day. Of course, my parents thought that I would go to sleep well before stumps each day. But they were wrong. How could anyone go to sleep while Victor Richardson and Alan McIlvray were describing a Test match against England!

Of course, as I found out later, that the ABC was not broadcasting live from England. They were in fact receiving a cable per ball from there, that cryptically described what had happened, and then they were making batting sounds and crowd noises to simulate an actual match. Clever devils that they were. But, to me, it probably would not have mattered had I known at the time. I was there, beneath three blankets with my crystal set, my ABC-Cricket book, and a pencil so that I could record every ball bowled. I still have that neat 1948 book, with all of its dots and runs, and for some reason, it is probably my most treasured possession.

But yes, the Invincibles. Remember them? The Third Test was spectacular. The Poms made a good fist of it. Before it was washed out on the last day, it looked like Australia would get the required runs, but it was not a sure thing. It was made unusual by the number of injuries that occurred. Dennis Compton, the English star batsman, was belted in the First Innings and again in the Second Innings. Both balls were from a fast bowler, and one hit him on the head, and the other on the body. These were the days before cricketers wore batting helmets, so the blows caused real concern. Washbrook, another Pom, was similarly hit, and damaged. Then Englishman Pollack cracked a long-hop to short mid-wicket, and it hit Sid Barnes in the kidneys. Barnes was fielding four yards from the bat, and he turned his back to the batsman, and so got the ball fair and square. He was taken from the field, but came in to bat next day. He batted bravely for thirty runs, and then collapsed at the crease, and was taken off again.

The highlight match of the tour was the Fourth Test. Again, England showed a bit of class, and got some runs in the First Innings. Australia replied with a poorish start, and was rescued by a great Century from left-hander Neil Harvey. This was a century in his first Ashes Test.

After that, Australia was left with 404 to get in its Second Innings on the last day. I would happily give you a ball-by-ball description of that day's play, but I suspect it might get too exciting for you. Suffice to say that the Aussies won, with twenty minutes to spare, and thus achieved the very rare feat of four hundred runs in a day. It was a great victory, the most memorable of the tour. For a 14-year-old boy, with his crystal set squeaking out its skinny signals, it was the most memorable ever.

Old-timers say the Pollard-Barnes injury was the worst ever seen in cricket, and they also say that this innings by Harvey was also about the best ever. Though, as an aside, I, now an old-timer, have to say that Adam Gilchrist in recent years has pinched that award in my book.

So, it was a great tour. The Aussies did not lose a match, and won the Tests handsomely. **Then came one of the greatest disasters in Test match history**. In the Fifth Test, when Don Bradman came in to bat, he needed just three runs in order to retire with a Test average of over a hundred. He came onto the ground, amid rapturous applause, and played one ball. The next ball, be was clean bowled. Out for a duck, for nil, for nothing. In his last Test innings. For the next twenty four hours, I died at regular intervals.

AUSSIE SPORT ON A WINNING STREAK

While all this was going on, Australia was doing well at other sports. In tennis, at Wimbledon, Frank Sedgman had suddenly hit the headlines. He had won the doubles, with John Bromwich, and was runner-up in the singles. This was almost the start of a glorious decade in which he and Ken McGregor dominated world tennis.

And, of course, our stars at the Olympic Games in Wembley, England, were policeman Merv Woods, who won gold in the sculling, and John Winter, who took the gold in the High Jump.

You would be right if you thought 1948 was a good year for Aussie sport.

NEWS AND VIEWS ON AUSSIE SPORTS

Suggestion for brighter cricket. At the end of the cricket season, the perennial question of how the rules should be changed in order to get "brighter" cricket, came up. The papers were full of answers, and as usual on this topic, the numbers of sensible and the number of ratbag answers were about equally balanced. This letter is fairly typical of the sensible ones, although maybe it does have a small element of ratbaggery in it

Letters, G Moyes. The best way to liven cricket is to make the bowlers' task easier, and curb the ultra-cautious tactics of batsmen with consequential piling up of mammoth scores.

After all, the most exciting games are those where the innings totals are moderate, say 200 to 250 runs each, not those with huge scores of 400 to 500 runs compiled after nearly two days' dull and painstaking play. I suggest increasing the height of the stumps by three or four inches, and the width by 25 per cent. Another suggestion to liven up the batting – it will be probably be howled down – would be for the umpires to declare a batsman out if he did not maintain a standard scoring rate after, say, 10 minutes playing himself in.

Tennis greats. At the end of the War, Australia found itself in a prominent position in world tennis. John Bromwich, Adrian Quist and Geoff Brown made quite a formidable team, and between them won more than their share of international events. Of course, a few years later they were swept aside by the world-beaters, Frank Sedgman and Ken McGregor.

But readers in 1948 were confronted with this far-from-successful anecdote about a small misfortune to John Bromwich.

Some may remember Bromwich's controversial habit of dropping the second tennis ball if he got his first serve in. On this particular occasion, after dropping the ball, Bromwich stood on it during the course of the rally, and suffered a nasty fall. He did, however, recover to win the match.

After this incident, the controversy went out of the issue, and players learned not to drop balls on courts.

The 'new' Butterfly stroke. Nancy Lyons, state **breaststroke** champion, announced that she would continue **her controversial new butterfly style at the Australian titles**. Although her times using this stroke were slower than usual, her coach decided she would persevere with the style. She did concede however, that if her times did not improve, she may revert to the conventional breaststroke style.

Comment. As this item reminds us, butterfly in the first instance, was just a new clever way of doing breaststroke, and was initially used by just a few swimmers in breaststroke races. As the technique was improved, and recorded times got better, it became necessary to split the events into two.

BIRTH OF PRINCE CHARLES

London, November 14th. It is with great pleasure that I announce the birth of a son to the Princess Elizabeth and her husband, Prince Phillip.

This long-awaited birth came more-or-less at the scheduled time, and produced a more-or-less normal baby, who was of course, subsequently named Charles. All of London, and indeed the British Empire, got itself into a tizz and guns were fired and drinkers got drunk.

Here in Australia, the people rejoiced, and made a fuss. All the normal congratulations poured forth from government and civic leaders, and it was generally conceded that it was a good thing that the new-born was a boy, because that in itself was a good thing, and the guns were fired at North Head as well.

Then the matter was wrapped up quickly in the Press. There was a series of baby photos and "Isn't he beautiful?" was asked a lot, rhetorically. The fuss went quickly. I suppose it is hard to keep up enthusiasm for a birth, even a royal birth. But still, that same Charles has survived, and is apparently thriving, even though he went through some personally difficult times.

Comment. He was born in London at 9.30pm on the 14th of November. It was reported in the British Press on the morning of the 15th. Due to the spinning of the earth, over which I no longer have much control, the Australian Papers reporting the birth were not printed until November 16th.

I was a bit sloppy and recorded the date in the First Edition of this book as November 16th. I perhaps should have recorded it as the 14th. In any case, I was told **that** by half a dozen readers who write amiable Letters to help me out.

The lesson I learned was, of course, to be more careful with my international dates. But more importantly, I realised just how many dedicated Royalists there were to whom the date of birth of the heir to the Throne was of considerable consequence.

There was very little thought of a Republican movement in this nation at this date.

DECEMBER NEWS ITEMS

Eighty British migrants will arrive by air next week from Britain. They will be **the first migrants to not come by sea**. They will arrive in **two charter flights that make it economical**. It is expected that soon many more will come by air, because **feeding them for about six weeks** on ships is a lot more expensive than for **five days** on flights.

The new Holden made its debut at a cocktail function at Sydney's Wentworth Hotel. Sydney's business world and social butterflies gathered in their formal evening gear, and sipped and gulped champagne, and disposed of an endless supply of hand-held munchies such as lobster mayonnaise. As three different-coloured models of the car revolved in centre hall, **a string orchestra played nostalgic melodies "that were sure to delight all ears."**

Australia's most popular man, **Don Bradman**, was photographed while strolling with King George VI on an informal visit to Buckingham Palace. At the time of the snap, **he had his hands in his pockets**....

The British press was up in arms against him for showing disrespect to the King....

Test cricketer Ian Johnson spoke for Australia when he pointed out that **the King often had both hands in pocket when speaking to Australian cricketers**. He pointed out that the King **at the time of the photo** also had one hand in a pocket....

Not good enough, replied the Press and several Royalists. The King was a special person, and **normal rules did not apply to him.**

On Tuesday December 13th, the **temperature** in the NSW town of **Cobar was 108 Degrees**.

Germany was devastated by the bombings and hostilities at the end of the war. **Many children were orphaned**, and the problem of what to do with them was **persisting**....

The Department of Immigration, under the guidance of Arthur Calwell, is **now proposing to bring out large numbers of these orphans.** He said that he would be the official guardian for them until they were **adopted by Australian families. If a child was not placed for any reason, it would be returned to Germany....**

Calwell might have had his heart in the right place in this instance but **more work needs to be done before this scheme would be viable.**

Remember pillion riding? The NSW Minister for Transport refused requests to ban it. He said that **it was no more dangerous than single-person riding**, and that safe-guards were in place. These included that the pillion rider must have his own footrests, and that a rider could pick up a pillion rider only after he had been legally riding for 12 months....

Comment. Mind you, my own experience was that **vast numbers of motor bike riders at this time had no thought of having any licence at all.**

SONG HITS FROM AMERICA

Buttons and Bows	Dinah Shaw
Cool Water	Vaughn Monroe
Gloria	Mills Brothers
What They Say About Dixie?	Al Jolson
Love Somebody	Doris Day
Twelfth Street Rag	Pee Wee Hunt
Underneath the Arches	Andrews Sisters
A Lovely Bunch Of Coconuts	Danny Kaye
On A Slow Boat To China	Kay Kayser

MOVIES RELEASED

Abbott and Costello Meet Frankenstein	Bud and Lou
Anna Karenina	Vivienne Leigh
Fort Apache	John Wayne
Hamlet	Sir Laurence Olivier
Johnny Belinda	Jayne Wyman
Easter Parade	Gene Kelly
The Three Musketeers	Gene Kelly
The Treasure of Sierra Madre	Humphrey Bogart
Oliver Twist	Alec Guinness

ACADEMY AWARDS

Best Actor, Laurence Olivier (Hamlet)
Best Actress, Jayne Wyman (Johnny Belinda)

SYDNEY LIVE THEATRE

On Saturday December 18th, there was plenty of live-theatre on sale in Sydney.

Opera was in the sixth week of a season at the Tivoli Theatre, long before the Opera House. *La Boheme* was currently on for a matinee, with *Rigoletto* for the evening. Over the next few weeks, *Barber of Seville*, *Madame Butterfly*, and *Pagliacci* were added to the programme, as were three other well-known operas. In all, it was a most comprehensive programme and, as I remember as a youth, absolutely brilliant to behold.

Not all audiences wanted so much sophistication, so there was a **modern English Variety Show** called *Take a Bow.* This starred *"Two-Ton"* Tessie O'Shea, billed as Britain's greatest singing comedienne.

For the children, there was a **pantomime** *Babes in the Woods.* This panto was a welcome sight because pantos had died out during the War, and the sight of men dressed as women and vice versa had been sorely missed.

There were plenty of **other stage shows**. *Annie Get Your Gun,* starring the popular Evie Hayes. The risque *Rusty Bugles* at North Sydney's Miller Street Theatre.

Shakespeare got a run in *Measure for Measure,* directed by Doris Fitton. And of course, **The Royal Philharmonic Society** of Sydney presented *The Messiah* on Christmas night at the Town Hall.

CATHOLIC DOGS – PERSONAL MEMORIES

Australia has always been lucky in the handling of its religious disputes. Lucky, that is, compared to other countries. Because, almost everywhere overseas, disputes between competing religions have been the cause of countless armed battles, murders, terrorist acts, and real enmities that sometimes spread over centuries. Luckily, I say, Australia has avoided these extreme forms of antagonism. But that is not to say bigotries and prejudices and rivalries did not exist in the Baby Boom years.

Let me start demonstrating this with a personal recollection of my school days in the mid-forties. Abermain was a small coal mining town with a population of two thousand people. At one end of the town was the Catholic school that I attended. It had 104 enrolled students and, because there were no cars, that fell away to 20 if it was raining hard. Up the other end of town were the Publics. Every day, on the way to and from school, little bands of Catholics passed similar groups of Publics. We always expressed rivalry and contempt for each other, but only occasionally were there any fisticuffs. But always Catholics, as we passed, would deliver with gusto this wonderfully constructed poetic masterpiece:

> Catholics, Catholics, ring the bell,
> While the Publics march to Hell.

Not to be denied, and with equal poetic merit, the Publics' rejoinder was:

> Catholic dogs jump like frogs,
> Eat no meat on Friday.

Looking back, it is easy to see these exchanges as trivial. But in fact, they were symptoms of **a real division in the community, between Catholics and Protestants**. There were no foreigners here, so race could not be divisive. Nor could riches, since there were no rich. Management always lived on colliery estates and so enmity with them was confined to the workplace. In short, our little community was quite homogeneous (to use today's word), and uniform - except for an enormous religious rift that always became apparent at the important moments in life.

I will illustrate this further with the description of how a number of likely couples were confronted with religious barriers to their marriages, over a period of many years.

I will start with Ben Chifley, and his ultimate bride, Elizabeth. This fine lady had an equally fine father, who was hard-working, quite prosperous, **a firm Presbyterian, and a Mason to boot**. In these latter two roles, **he was quite antagonistic to Catholics**, and this meant that when young Ben Chifley wanted to marry his daughter, he strongly opposed the marriage. Not on any personal grounds, for he and Ben were both engine drivers, and worked quite well together. It was the Catholicity that was the problem.

So Ben, in 1914, was forced to make the decision between his faith and his choice of a life-long partner. "Mixed marriages" such as this had been forbidden by the Catholic Church since 1908, so he made a choice in favour of the girl. He was married in Sydney, away from his home town of Bathurst, in the Presbyterian Church, without the presence of Elizabeth's parents. He did continue to practice his Catholicity, while she remained true to her faith.

Now here I must pause to say that I do not in any way wish to compare myself to the great and much-beloved Ben Chifley. But it is appropriate to point out that forty years later, in 1956, my own wedding was almost identical. Here I was then, a young Uni graduate with a good job, courting a beautiful Presbyterian girl, who happened to have a father who was a Mason. So it happened all over again, except that we married in her home church in Weston, and all parents were thankfully there.

I must say that when I was confronted by this marital dilemma in 1956, I was quite cavalier about it. **Surely**, mixed marriages were not a problem in this day and age. **Surely**, all those bigotries from before the turn of the century, or even before the War, no longer plagued us. I soon found out that they did. In fact they were in no way diminished. I should have realised this because, back in Abermain, the school kids were still chanting the same verses at each other every day.

Surely there was a way round it all. I went, with my fiancée, to visit the Sydney University Catholic Chaplain. What could be done? He liked talking in the vernacular of the students, so he replied "not a bloody thing", and gave his big friendly trade-mark smile that sort of said "there, that's settled, go away and be happy." At the time there were a number of Filipino priests touting for business as priests without parishes, and who were reputedly breaking our rules that **they** claimed were foisted on us by our Irish bishops. Could I first get married in the Presbyterian Church, and then do a back door job with one of these itinerants?

Again in the vernacular, "not a hope in hell." Any variation from the norm would mean I would be excommunicated.

So my decision was easy. On the one hand, I had the entire Catholic Church, with one billion followers, positively salivating, so I thought at the time, for me to step out of line. On the other hand, there was this beautiful girl. Of course, for a healthy vigorous young man, it was an unequal contest. So we were married a few months later in the Presbyterian Church.

Sad to say, a few years later, another couple, my friends, had a different ending. He was initially a Christian Brothers monk, and later a schoolteacher in a large private school, and she was a solicitor, in the days when there were not too many ladies thus employed. The outcome here was that neither would or could budge, so that they broke up. I do not know what happened to the lady, but he has remained for fifty years without a partner, something that plagues him daily. Now he is old, and getting infirm, he sorrowfully repeats what he used to say as a joke "I would be better off back in the Christian Brothers."

Other manifestations. Of course, **religious intolerance** was not restricted to weddings. It popped up everywhere. I will give you five examples.

Firstly. My father had been born of good Irish stock into the Catholic Church, and attended a Catholic school until he was thirteen. But he had no allegiance to the Church; in fact – horror, horror – even when the terrifying Redemptrist missionaries came to town every two or three years, he never attended.

Davie Haunter lived down on the corner, he was a retired person who kept to himself, except once a month he would get drunk on port on a Sunday afternoon, and come looking for an argument. And before you knew it, it turned into a religious argument.

Now, my father knew nothing at all about religion, and he cared even less about it. But somehow, the Haunter approach of blaming all the problems of the world on Catholics got his goat, and for ten minutes, until the port called Haunter again, he was the fiercest crusader you would ever see. So, the two of them would argue. There was a lot of very loud talk, and no one ever got to finish a sentence. In the very quick long run, it always got down to the famous scapegoats of history. King Henry VIII, the immoral Protestant, had eight (yes, eight) wives. The Catholic Barnabas the Fictitious was a drunk and had it off with animals. On a Sunday. It was a good show, great to watch. But it was quite typical of the times, when uninformed people would argue and argue over religious issues that weren't even issues.

Secondly, Abermain was a mining town set in an agricultural setting. On one side of the town was acreage suitable for grazing dairy cows. Quite a few people, anxious to stay alive, had their own beast, and they pastured in a 200-acre paddock owned by a Mr Stanley Tennament. This latter person was a true product of the land, was commonly regarded as having a "red" temper, and was prone to engage in the violent religious arguments described above. The problem for some of us was that, every few months, he lost an argument so badly that he felt aggrieved enough to use his ultimate weapon against Catholics. So he would get on his horse, ride round to all his Catholic lessees, and tell them to "take your bloody Catholic cows out of my paddock." A few days later he would repent and the cows would go back in. My mother always wanted a refund for days when the cow was out. But she could make no headway against the forceful logic in his reply "I'll not give you money that you'll send those mongrels in Rome."

Thirdly. *The Rock* was a tabloid weekly newspaper that appeared in the late forties. It was a 12-page diatribe based on nothing other than the atrocities that Catholics had and were committing. No one in our parish paid any intention to it, until one Sunday our local priest came to the Sunday Mass in an obvious rage. So great a rage, in fact, that he gave the sermon before the actual Mass itself. Instead of in the middle. He just could not contain himself.

His outrage stemmed from the fact the *The Rock* had reported on a matter that impacted his diocese, and indeed by some paranoid inference, even extended to his parish. His fury was evident; no swearing of course, but sluts, vermin, mongrels, prostitutes, gutless, and bitches featured prominently. He swore "by God" that any one who ever read *The Rock*, (and suddenly the *Miners' Federation Weekly*), would be instantly excommunicated and "would haunt the halls of Hell forever." It was a complete rave that, I am happy to say, was not quite typical of the time; but it does show the passions that were aroused in some poor tortured souls by religious attacks. In passing, I mention that at the end of Mass, he enjoined us, as usual, to go in peace.

Fourthly. Back to a wedding theme. This time I want to look at a wedding from the viewpoint of a guest. My first cousin, Jackie, was a town hero, because he was the world's fastest Rugby League winger. He would admit that at any time. He was a practising Catholic, and after the normal heart-wrenching decision, he decided to marry Gwen in the Church of England. I was a 12-year old, an altar boy, and devout to the point of lunacy. So the Church said I could not attend the ceremony. This became a very real problem for me. It was the first time I questioned the teachings of Mother Church. I reasoned that there was no harm done if I went, that everyone else was going; and would it start the drift away from Catholicity in the nation that Mother Church obviously feared?

In any case, I skulked outside the Church for the ceremony, and was happy to join the reception afterwards. But, once again, it was a sign of how rigidly the rules of religions were enforced, and how society was segregated into unarmed camps, for the love of God. It was all pretty silly.

Fifthly, the town cricket team. Sturdy blacksmiths and police constables mixed on our village green to smite deadly blows with the willow, and visitors blanched with terror as our living legends dished out the punishment. The trouble for me was that these giants of cricket were all Protestant. They had been for years, and while it was accepted that a Catholic could come for training, there was no hope that he could join the august Eleven. The remarkable thing about this was that it was just accepted. No complaints, no resentment. It was just what had been done for years, and was now simply the done thing.

Well now, 70 years later, I am told by many, the situation has improved. Religion is not the divisive force that it once was, the churches are ecumenical, and they share many ceremonies and situations. This to me is a good thing. I must say I am not quite convinced. Just look at the web-site for the Catholic Church regarding the rules for marriage. You will see that it is still pretty severe, and it does not seem to offer much scope for mixed marriages.

But, no, I give in to the majority and accept that, in practice, things are better. I would know for sure if I could hear the school children chanting as they passed each other on the way to school. Do Catholic dogs still jump like frogs? I guess I will never know, because they now pass each other in cars, so their words of wisdom remain unspoken.

But I am sure that religion has **not** gone away completely **as a divisive issue**. The good people of the Middle East have now (in 2018) become the bogies for some in our community. For these latter, **our God is infinitely better than their God**, and our people are infinitely better than their people. I wonder **if** we can clear up this misunderstanding in a hundred years, will we find another variation to keep us happy for the next hundred. I just do not know. Do you?

SUMMING UP 1948

As I look back at what I have written for 1948, I think three major themes come through.

First, though not so clearly enunciated, the country was in the grip of prosperity. Jobs were plentiful, crops were good, and mining and manufacturing were picking up. People were generally happy with their lot. They were forming families, buying houses, and even cars, electric lawn mowers, and washing machines. Bank loans could be got if you crawled low enough, sport was all happening, and beer and knitting wool could sometimes be bought. Things were not perfect, but they were better than they had been, and looked better for the future.

Second, the Chifley government was in trouble. It was losing its battle to convert Australia to socialism, it had lost its price control mandate, had failed in it banking ambitions, and was plagued with a nation that was repeatedly blaming Communists for all the strikes, and at the same time, some of the blame rubbed off onto Labor. It was not obvious at the time, but it is easy to see one group after another being alienated by Labor's policy, and when you add that to the petrol fiasco and the miners'strike of 1949, Labor's defeat in the elections of that year was inevitable.

Third. The Reds everywhere were becoming a genuine worry in the Western world. At home, they were involved in strike after strike. Granted, many of these strikes would have happened without them, because after all, they were a legal method of bargaining, and it was a period when workers were striving for increased shares of business profits, and better working conditions. But the Communists were so consistent, and their patterns of strikes were so disruptive, that clearly some of them were tying themselves to goals that would lead to the overthrow of capitalism, as in Russia. So, they were unpopular in 1948, and became more so over the next few years, as Menzies progressively milked the Communist cow for all he could.

Overseas, the Communists were everywhere, and in most places it was clear that they were intent on subversion of the existing governments. Right through South-East Asia, they were tied in with the forces that were seeking to remove the colonial powers of yesteryear, and they were prominent in rebellions in all those States. They were to become of greater significance to us as the years passed. Elsewhere they were getting as much power as they could, some by fair means, and many more by foul means, and in this they were matched step for step by the Americans.

Apart from those themes, life went on pretty well. The Baby Boom gathered momentum, though no one had any idea that it would be as strong and enduring as it turned out to be. Most people thought that it was just a post-war blip. In fact, there was much talk at the time about how **we must populate or perish**, and immigration programmes were now in place that saw us import 100,000 migrants a year or more. Many of these were from the European mainland, and so the concentration of British blood began to reduce. But our loyalty to the British peoples, and the Royal family, remained mostly steadfast. The engagement and the marriage of Elizabeth had been hugely interesting to people here, and the Royal Tour next year was expected to be an enormous success.

So, life was almost back to normal. Even all those irritating price controls had been beaten. There were no major causes such as wars and poverty and a Depression to make people worry. Folks were simply getting on with living, breeding, and otherwise having fun. They had the wherewithal to do that, and they were surrounded by other people who were in the same frame of mind. In all, it was a good year, and a good time was had by almost all.

READERS' COMMENTS

Tom Lynch, Speers Point. Some history writers make the mistake of trying to boost their authority by including graphs and charts all over the place. You on the other hand get a much better effect by saying things like "he made a pile". Or "every one worked hours longer than they should have, and felt like death warmed up at the end of the shift." I have seen other writers waste two pages of statistics painting the same picture as you did in a few words.

Barry Marr, Adelaide You know that I am being facetious when I say that I wish the war had gone on for years longer so that you would have written more books about it.

Edna College, Auburn. A few times I stopped and sobbed as you brought memories of the postman delivering letters, and the dread that ordinary people felt as he neared. How you captured those feelings yet kept your coverage from becoming maudlin or bogged down is a wonder to me.

Betty Kelly, Wagga Wagga. Every time you seem to be getting serious, you throw in a phrase or memory that lightens up the mood. In particular, in the war when you were describing the terrible carnage of Russian troops, you ended with a ten-line description of how aggrieved you felt and ended it with "apart from that, things are pretty good here". For me, it turned the unbearable into the bearable, and I went from feeling morbid and angry back to a normal human being.

Alan Davey, Brisbane. I particularly liked the light-hearted way you described the scenes at the airports as American, and British, high-flying entertainers flew in. I had always seen the crowd behaviour as disgraceful, but your light-hearted description of it made me realise it was in fact harmless and just good fun.

MORE INFORMATION ON THESE BOOKS

Over the past 15 years the author, Ron Williams, has written this series of books that present a social history of Australia in the post-war period. They cover the period for 1939 to 1968, with one book for each year. Thus there are 30 books.

To capture the material for each book, the author, Ron Williams, worked his way through the *Sydney Morning Herald* and the *Age/Argus* day-by-day, and picked out the best stories, ideas and trivia. He then wrote them up into 176 pages of a year-book.

He writes in a direct conversational style, he has avoided statistics and charts, and has produced easily-read material that is entertaining, and instructive, and charming.

They are invaluable as gifts for birthdays, Christmas, and anniversaries, and for the oldies who are hard to buy for.

These books are available at all major retailers. They are listed also in all leading catalogues, including Title Page and Dymocks and Booktopia.

22569018R00102

Printed in Great Britain
by Amazon